MEET THE ANCESTORS

MEET THE ANCESTORS

Unearthing the evidence
that brings us face to face with the past

JULIAN RICHARDS

For my Mum, my wife Sue
and my son Barnaby

FRONTISPIECE: *Meeting an ancestor – the author at work
on a 1300-year-old grave.*

This book is published to accompany the television series
Meet the Ancestors, of which the first series was originally
broadcast on BBC 2 in 1997 and the second series in 1999.
Executive producer: Caroline van den Brul
Series producer: Ian Potts
Producers: Paul Bradshaw, Siân Griffiths

Published by BBC Worldwide Ltd,
80 Wood Lane, London W12 0TT

First published in 1999
© Julian Richards 1999
The moral right of the author has been asserted

ISBN 0 563 38458 1

Commissioning editor: Sheila Ableman
Project editor: Martha Caute
Text editor: Christine King
Art director: Linda Blakemore
Designer: Martin Hendry
Illustrator: Jane Brayne

Set in Garamond No. 3
Printed and bound in France by Imprimerie Pollina s.a.
Colour separations by Radstock Reproductions Ltd,
Midsomer Norton
Jacket printed by Imprimerie Pollina s.a.

CONTENTS

INTRODUCTION

WHAT FIRST FASCINATED me about archaeology was finding things, objects that were 200 or even 2000 years old and which had lain in the ground unseen since they had been lost or thrown away. I remember clearly the first excavation I ever went on, in my home town of Nottingham, and the amused reaction of more seasoned diggers as I enthused about even the tiniest scraps of pottery. That fascination has remained with me – I can still appreciate the craft that has gone into the making of a fine flint arrowhead or the decoration of a bronze brooch. Somewhere along the line, though, I started to realize that archaeology wasn't just about objects, or about ruins and monuments: it was about people. People had built and lived in the castle we were uncovering, had dug out and filled the rubbish pit that I was busy re-excavating, and someone, a real person, had made and used the pot that I now held in smashed fragments. At the time this was a revelation to me: the past was peopled and suddenly it seemed a much friendlier place.

It was five years after that first excavation, in my first job as a full-time archaeologist in Berkshire, that I came face to face with someone from the past. There had been some winter gales, and in the little village of Upper Lambourn an old beech tree had blown down at the bottom of a cottage garden. The owners got a terrible shock when they went to inspect the damage – grinning from the tangled roots of the fallen tree was a human skull. The local police were the first on the scene, but they soon lost interest when they realized that the tree had been there for at least 100 years and consequently there was no crime to solve. That's when I was called in. As I prised the skull from the tree roots and cleared away more soil to find the rest of the bones, it became clear that what I was uncovering was not just a skeleton: it was all that remained of one of those people I had started to become so fascinated with. This person, a woman, had lived close to this place towards the end of the Roman period, over 1600 years ago. Who was she? And who were the two men she was buried with, whose remains lay within the huge hole torn out by the tree roots? Together, these people may have farmed the fields that I had been tracing and mapping from aerial photographs; they must have known the Roman villa that I had discovered as a scatter of tiles in a nearby ploughed field. This was probably the moment when the seed for *Meet the Ancestors* was sown.

Over the following twenty years I excavated many sites and uncovered many burials. Prehistoric skeletons

The first skeleton I ever encountered, a Roman man from Upper Lambourn in Berkshire. For over 1600 years he lay undisturbed deep in the chalk until a freak storm blew down the tree that had guarded his grave in more recent centuries.

crouched under burial mounds high on the chalk downs seemed to belong to people from such a remote past that it was difficult to imagine their lives. It was easier to imagine the life, and death, of the men hastily buried after a Civil War battle and who turned up under someone's kitchen extension. Some, like the child buried close to Stonehenge in a grave so large that it made the tiny skeleton look even smaller and more vulnerable, had a profound effect on the way I felt about excavating burials. I have regretted excavating that child's burial ever since, and would feel much happier if I could replace the young bones where they were first buried over 3000 years ago.

The idea that these people were all our ancestors crystallized for me on a site in a gravel pit near Cirencester. We had unexpectedly uncovered a few graves, lying on the edge of the Roman farmstead where the people must have lived. There is something about skeletons that always excites curiosity and many of the local villagers came to see what we had found. As they gazed down on the bones I was suddenly struck with the idea that these skeletons, over 1500 years old, could be their ancestors. Until quite recently many people did not move far from their birthplace, and there seemed no reason why the farmers of today could not be the descendants of the farmers of Roman times. I didn't suggest this idea to our visitors at the time – I am sure that they might well have ridiculed the idea that these burials were anything to do with them. To most of us the idea of our ancestry does not go back beyond faded family photographs or, at the very most, a search through parish records of births, marriages and deaths. This may take us back a few centuries, but beyond that? My grandparents could remember Queen Victoria's Jubilee in 1897, while their great-grandparents were born at the end of the eighteenth century. On that reckoning it is fewer than forty generations back to the Norman Conquest in 1066, sixty to our Roman farmers and no more than eighty to the birth of Christ. Suddenly time seems to shrink.

In a deep grave near Stonehenge the crouched skeleton of a Bronze Age child looks very small and vulnerable. This is a grave that I have always regretted disturbing.

If these burials really are of our ancestors, then our ancestors lie all around us. Since the arrival of Christianity many of the dead have been buried in familiar places – consecrated ground such as churchyards, crypts and great urban cemeteries. But those that came before often lie in what appear to us today to be the most unexpected spots. Maybe this is because we see the landscape in a different way from our pagan ancestors. To most of us hills and valleys, woods and streams are part of the 'scenery'; to them the land provided the means of survival and within those woods and streams were sacred places where the gods dwelt. Their burial places were chosen with care, to be visible, to mark a boundary or to be near the gods, but over time their meaning has often been forgotten.

It is not surprising, then, that each year throughout the British Isles hundreds, and sometimes thousands, of human burials are

LEFT: *Ernest and Ethel Parker, my grandparents on my mother's side of the family, pictured in 1913. For many of us family photographs and the odd faded document are our only link to our ancestors.*

RIGHT: *One of the great municipal cemeteries established in the nineteenth century in many of our towns and cities to cope with the problems of churchyards overflowing with graves.*

unearthed. Sometimes they emerge unexpectedly in the bucket of a mechanical digger, but more often than not these days their discovery is predicted by archaeologists. Marks on aerial photographs can show the site of a flattened burial mound; finds made centuries ago can point to areas of interest; and the names of fields or tracks, like 'Bone Lane', can provide useful clues. Whatever the circumstances of discovery, in every case the disturbance of human remains must be reported to the coroner and their removal must be licensed by the Home Office.

These then were the ingredients for *Meet the Ancestors*: the fact that the British Isles is one huge graveyard and that each year for a wide variety of reasons lots of burials are excavated; and, finally, an awareness that modern science could tell us a lot about people, not only the way they lived and died, but even how they might have looked. For

an archaeologist like me, whose reconstructions of past people up to this time had always borne an uncanny resemblance to colleagues of the right gender and age, the revelation that faces from the past could indeed be re-created opened a whole new area of fascination and investigation. This was going to provide us with the means of literally 'meeting' our ancestors.

The delicately balanced stones of a prehistoric tomb in Cornwall mark the hilltop burial place of a select few. Chosen with care for their prominence, these burial places were designed to enhance the status of the dead.

So how did we go about arranging these meetings? First we contacted every archaeologist in the British Isles, in museums, universities and digging organizations, and asked them if they were planning any excavations which might involve examining burials. If they were, could we come along and record their work? At first it seemed as if everyone we contacted had just finished excavating the most fascinating burials, and I began to get quite worried as I heard the phrase, 'It's a pity you weren't doing this

last year,' for the fifth time in a day. But then we started to hear about sites that were just about to be dug, unexpected discoveries were made, and suddenly I was off in my Land Rover on a summer-long gallop from the Lake District to Wiltshire, back home to Dorset and from Suffolk to the Atlantic coast of Donegal in Eire.

The location of all the sites was simply a matter of what turned up and of which archaeological organizations invited us to become involved in their excavations. The apparent bias towards southern England is not through any desire to work close to home (the second series also includes a site in Orkney) but a result of several factors. There are whole areas of the British Isles, most of the southwest peninsula for example and many clayey or highland areas, where the soils are too acidic for bone to survive. In addition, there are greater pressures for development within southern England which result in a greater number of archaeological investigations.

This book contains the stories of the five sites we investigated for the first series of *Meet the Ancestors*, together with four from our second series excavated early enough in our filming schedule to provide sufficient details. Everywhere we met committed and friendly archaeologists, willing to share their sites and their enthusiasm with us and with the viewers. This was archaeology as it really happens, with all its fascination and frustration.

As an archaeologist who has spent more time behind a desk than a wheelbarrow over the past few years, it was great to be back on site, helping out when I could and rediscovering muscles and aches that I had forgotten about. One aspect of archaeology that I hadn't forgotten about was its unpredictability. You can go to a site with a reasonable idea of what is going to be there only to be proved horribly wrong when the turf starts to come off. This happened to us a few times. There was the Iron Age cemetery which seemed to hold exciting possibilities until we found that it had all been quarried away in the last century. There was the Roman cemetery which, after the topsoil was stripped off over 2 acres, produced only one burial, and that was of a pig. Then there was the Bronze Age burial mound, perched on the edge of a spectacular Sussex cliff, which turned out to have been robbed by an unknown antiquarian some time in the last century. But, in among the disappointments, there were some wonderful sites and finds.

Although each excavation finished with the removal of the buried bones, in many ways this was just the start of the investigation into these past lives. The remains of each individual were tracked around the country to be examined by expert after expert. Experience, medical knowledge, microscopes, X-rays, computers and isotopes all added to the evolving picture of nine individuals, each with their own story to tell. Their tales included hints of childhood starvation and the effects of a lifetime of hard manual labour. Their bones gave clues to their diet and to where they were born. But perhaps the most remarkable part of the picture was the way in which their faces emerged as experts breathed life back into the ancient and often shattered skulls.

Our facial reconstruction specialists, Richard Neave and Robin Richards, use two very different methods to achieve their remarkable results. Richard and his team of medical artists used clay and a sculptural technique to translate their anatomical expertise into four of our ancestral faces. With their experience in rebuilding shattered and fragmentary skulls, they were well able to take up the challenge of our most damaged and incomplete specimens. Robin harnesses the power of computers to map and merge, creating an individual mask which then requires a human touch. This is where the artistry of our illustrator Jane Brayne proved so valuable. Jane's ability to humanize the five faces generated by Robin's computer brought us closer to these particular ancestors. And on some of our sites she was also able to re-create for us the landscape that they would have known and within which they spent their lives.

All this is what has enabled us to *Meet the Ancestors*...

Crowlink barrow, poised on the cliff edge near Beachy Head in Sussex. A Bronze Age burial mound like this seemed to offer a good chance of meeting one of our ancestors until we discovered that it had been robbed over 100 years ago.

THE ULTIMATE SACRIFICE

THERE ARE PARTS of the British Isles where it is easier to feel close to the distant past, where burial mounds dot the hilltops and ancient ditches trace lines and circles, the purpose of which has long been forgotten. Cranborne Chase is one such place, a huge area of rolling chalk downland spanning the borders of Hampshire, Wiltshire and Dorset, and bounded on two sides by the rivers Stour and Avon. Now an ordered and cultivated landscape, small pockets of grassland and woods hint at its use in past centuries when royal hunting parties came to the Chase for their sport.

Martin Green is a farmer in the Chase, with 260 acres at Down Farm near the little village of Sixpenny Handley in Dorset. His farm has its share of mounds and ditches and these hints of an ancient landscape excited Martin's curiosity from a young age. He found his first flint arrowhead in the grounds of his primary school and from then on his winters were spent 'fieldwalking', scouring the surface of ploughed fields for more flint tools and fragments of pottery. As Martin's collection grew, so did his curiosity and eventually he could not resist trying to find out what lay below the surface of these flinty chalk fields. The first small excavations produced volumes of ancient finds and happily coincided with the bottom falling out of the egg market. The old hen house was converted into the 'Gussage and District Museum', and from then on it was always a matter of debate whether Martin was a farmer with an interest in archaeology or an archaeologist who happened to have a farm. Excavations and field-walking were fitted into the annual farming cycle and acquaintance with a local light plane pilot suddenly gave a new perspective to the landscape.

Those of us who know Martin have got used to the unexpected. It seems as if every site that he investigates, if not unique, has something distinctly odd about it. The site he excavated in 1997 was to prove no exception to this rule. The year before, hanging over the side of a friend's microlight aircraft, Martin had noted some strange pale marks showing in a crop of peas on a farm belonging to one of his neighbours. The soils in this field, which lies on the crest of a low ridge, are thin and chalky and the contrasts in the growth of the crop were caused by places where the plants could send their roots down deeper, gathering up stored water and nutrients. A regular circle of pale spots surrounded a large central blob and to Martin it looked like a 'henge', a ceremonial timber circle dating to the Neolithic period, possibly as far back as 2500 BC. Martin had already excavated a number of sites of Neolithic date and, like anyone who has been involved with this period, when ritual and ceremony formed such an important part of everyday life, was fascinated by it. Spanning the years between about 4000 and 2000 BC, farming of both animals and crops gradually replaced the old ways of hunting and gathering. As the old nomadic life changed and people became more settled, so they gathered together to create extraordinary earthen sculptures: long burial mounds, hilltop camps with many entrances, timber circles enfolded by deep ditches and, perhaps strangest of all, long thin 'cursus' monuments. These are parallel ditches and banks which stride for miles across the countryside, beginning and ending at places of burial and maybe of astronomical significance.

It is quite easy to excavate on your own land, but neighbours need to be persuaded, even though they are all used to Martin's obsessions.

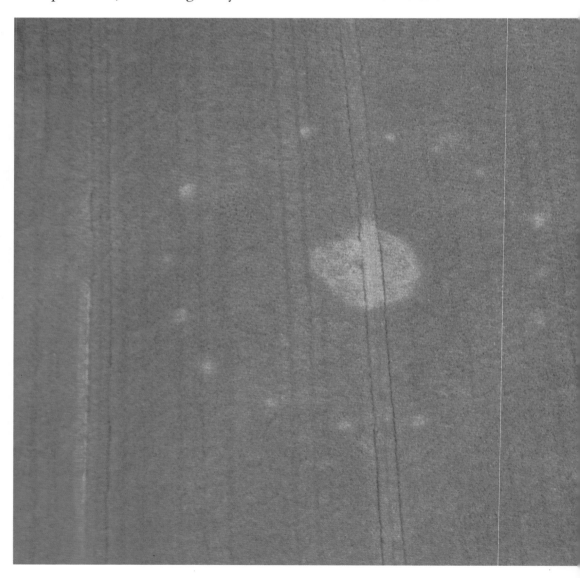

Martin was very keen to find out what he could about this site, and eventually an agreement was reached which gave him the site to investigate and a route to it through the growing crop. When the topsoil was stripped off, the pattern seen from the air was confirmed. Within the great expanse of gleaming white chalk, the dark spots seen from the air showed up even more clearly as brown soil-filled pits, unevenly spaced and arranged in a rough oval. The circuit was

LEFT: *Pale marks in a crop of peas, spotted by Martin on this aerial photograph, led him to another unique site. The small pale dots represented a circle of pits which surround an unusual central hollow. The circle in the top right corner is a small ploughed down Bronze Age burial mound of which only its surrounding ditch can now be seen.*

RIGHT: *Martin Green, farmer and archaeologist, at work on the site of his latest discovery.*

not complete – to the east and west were wider gaps, maybe suggesting that these were entrances, the ways in to what lay in the centre.
The circular patch of soil that lay within the oval of pits was over 12
metres in diameter and, almost as soon as Martin started to excavate
it, provided the first surprise of the excavation.

In the exact centre of the soil patch, not far below the present surface, lay a small, neat heap of flint cobbles, rough, unshaped, the sort
that can be gathered from the surface of any ploughed field on the
Chase. As Martin unpicked the heap, flint by flint, bones appeared
and as more flints were removed so more bones were added until eventually a complete skeleton was revealed. At first glance the skeleton
appeared to be of a male and he was affectionately named 'Adam'. He
lay on his side, with his head facing east, out through one of the
entrances in the outer oval of pits. When had he been buried? Nothing was found with him, but close by were fragments of pottery and
distinctive flint arrowheads dating back to the early part of the
Bronze Age, about 1700 BC. With one unexpected burial on his site
and maybe more to come, Martin contacted *Meet the Ancestors* and this
is where our involvement began.

When we first arrived on site, driving along the narrow track left
through the field of ripening corn, it was immediately obvious why
the site had been built in this place. The ridge gave clear views to the
west, over burial mounds and henges, and towards where something
very strange undulated across the hills and valleys and through
Martin's farm: the Dorset Cursus, an enclosure formed by ditches and
banks, 100 metres wide and nearly 10 kilometres long. It was built
nearly 5000 years ago and seems to have acted like a magnet, attract-
ing to it the builders of some equally strange sites, one of which it
seemed as if Martin had found.

Adam had not been buried in a proper grave, merely laid out on
the ground in the centre of what must have been a shallow circular
hollow and covered with flints. As a result, some of his bones were in
a very poor state. His skull in particular, vital if we were to be able to

reconstruct his face with any confidence, was crushed quite badly and it was obvious that any attempt to remove it would result in complete collapse. It needed to come out in a solid block of soil, and help came from the Conservation Laboratory in Salisbury. We weren't quite sure how they were going to approach the problem and it was quite alarming to see the skull first covered in silver foil, very science fiction, before being covered in liquid rubber. This looked more like a skull again but then it was packed around with fine soil, a metal plate was slid underneath it and finally it was bandaged for transport. It ending up looking like a badly made wedding cake.

Stripped of their masking soil, the pits visible on the aerial photograph show clearly as darker patches in the white chalk. Wider gaps in the circle of pits suggest opposed entrances leading into the central hollow.

With Adam safely removed and his bones back in the laboratory of Wessex Archaeology where they would be cleaned for detailed examination, we left Martin to carry on the excavation, promising to return shortly to see what the big central hole turned out to be. He had assured us that it wouldn't be much deeper as he had bored down

into it before he started digging, narrowly missing Adam's skull, and had hit solid chalk at a depth of just over 1 metre. This was only in part of it, though. When we next visited the site, Martin's Land Rover was parked by the spoil heap and Abi the retriever was tied up in her usual place digging holes just like her master. There was no sign of Martin, and when we got closer we could see why. Cut into one side of the now emptied central hollow was a huge circular shaft, dug down nearly 7 metres into the chalk. Martin had emptied the shaft of the chalk rubble and soil that had gradually filled it over the millennia and now, near its base, the marks of the tools used by the prehistoric miners could clearly be seen. The chalk had been hacked and prised

LEFT: *'Adam', a Bronze Age man. His burial, under a low mound of flints in the centre of the site, marked the last use of the grave pit.*

RIGHT: *From deep in the shaft came this strange decorated chalk block, its designs echoing those found carved inside ancient Neolithic stone tombs.*

out using picks of red deer antler, broken fragments of which lay within the chalk rubble, then trimmed more neatly with axes of polished flint or stone. Constructing this shaft must have been an enormous task, digging out tons of chalk by hand, but what was its purpose? Could any of the objects that it contained provide the clues? Deep in the rubble filling Martin had found cattle bones, but some were from cattle unlike any that we know today. These were from aurochs, long-extinct giant cattle. Lower down the shaft was a smoothed block of chalk, a socket carved into one side, the surfaces of the others decorated with elaborate carved spirals and lines, just like those found on the walls of ancient stone tombs in Ireland and Scotland. But none of these explained why the shaft had been dug and the only time that any of us felt that we were close to any understanding of its purpose was when we climbed down the ladder and stood at its base. Here, looking up at a perfect circle of blue sky, there was a real feeling of being part of the earth. Perhaps this was why it was dug, to get closer to the gods of the earth, deep down where the precious flint could be found.

The shaft had been cut through the base of the large central hollow which, as we examined it more closely, had obviously been very carefully dug. Its shape was remarkably regular, its sides near to vertical, and its floor when first exposed had an almost polished appearance as if worn smooth by trampling feet. Again we were left puzzling what could have caused this, what dances or rituals could have worn this floor so smooth. On the floor of the hollow was a low curved bank, running around part of the lip of the great shaft. It seemed to be built out of some of the chalk rubble from the first digging of the shaft and Martin had found it quite useful as a safety

The great shaft, dug deep into the chalk through the base of the large central hollow and surrounded by a low rubble bank.

barrier. This might have been its original purpose, to stop curious visitors getting too close to the edge of the shaft, but as it was gradually removed it revealed its own secret. Tucked under the edge of the large central hollow was a small oval chalk-filled pit, so difficult to see that it almost seemed as if attempts had been made to conceal it. The upper levels were of hard-packed small fragments of chalk which looked little different to the surrounding undisturbed bedrock, but underneath was a layer of large chalk blocks. As the first of these was prised out Martin peered into the void, and what he saw was not the white of chalk but the pale yellow brown of bone, the top of a skull. I don't think that I have ever seen Martin so excited. 'I know how Howard Carter felt when he looked into the tomb of Tutankhamun!' was his first reaction. It took a little while for the implications of this new find to sink in. There was a burial in the pit and because it lay in the earliest levels of the site it had to be much older than Adam. Suddenly he seemed to be a mere youngster at less than 4000 years old.

We watched and emptied buckets as, on a showery day, Martin removed more of the chalk blocks, expecting to see more of the skeleton gradually appear. What none of us expected was a second skull. At the same end of the oval pit, nestling close to the first one and facing in the same direction, the familiar dome of yellow bone appeared through the chalk. Martin decided that this was quite enough excitement for one day and moved to the other end of the pit, where the feet should be. But there were no feet, just a third skull and then a fourth, these two facing the original pair. As if to signal this amazing discovery the sun came out and a spectacular rainbow appeared over the site. By this time our imagination was running riot. Maybe these were not burials, maybe the pit was just full of skulls – after all, wherever Martin had looked so far that was all he had found.

We watched as more of the blocks were removed, and then the smaller pieces of crushed chalk. Gradually a mass of bones was exposed, a leg bone, some toes, ribs and arms, the curved shape of a disjointed spine. Finally, after hours spent hanging head down in the pit, Martin stood back and we could see the outlines of four skeletons, two at each end of the pit, each tightly crouched as if asleep. The bones of each pair were jumbled, as if their bodies when placed in the pit had been huddled together, and we realized, as we stared at this extraordinary sight, that three of the skeletons were very small — they were of children. No matter how many ancient burials you have dealt with, and how professionally detached you are supposed to be, there is always something about a child's grave which provokes feelings of great sadness. Young life was terribly fragile in the past but the loss of a child would have been no less of a tragedy in prehistoric times than it is today.

It was obvious as we looked at the bones, lying on the base of their grave pit, that the three children, and the one adult who lay with them, had been placed in the grave as bodies, not as collections of bones. This meant that they had all died and been buried at the same time. What did this mean? Was this a family tragedy, mother and three children all struck down together, perhaps by some disease or plague? Or was there a more sinister reason, one which archaeologists are perhaps unwilling at times to contemplate? Were these people sacrificed at the time that this strange site was first built, killed and buried in a concealed grave in the base of the pit that was to see the trampling of many feet before its meaning was eventually lost? The answers to our questions were only going to come from a detailed examination of the bones and so, after Martin had drawn and photographed the contents of the grave, the preparations were made to remove them.

Jackie McKinley is Wessex Archaeology's human-bone specialist, and it was her job to try to disentangle the bones and identify to which individual each separate bone belonged. Each bone, as it was removed, was identified and placed in a separate labelled bag. 'Burial A, right femur', 'Burial C, left clavicle' assured that when back at the laboratory, each skeleton could be reassembled. This is a slow and painstaking task, and is not helped by rain, so when the showers

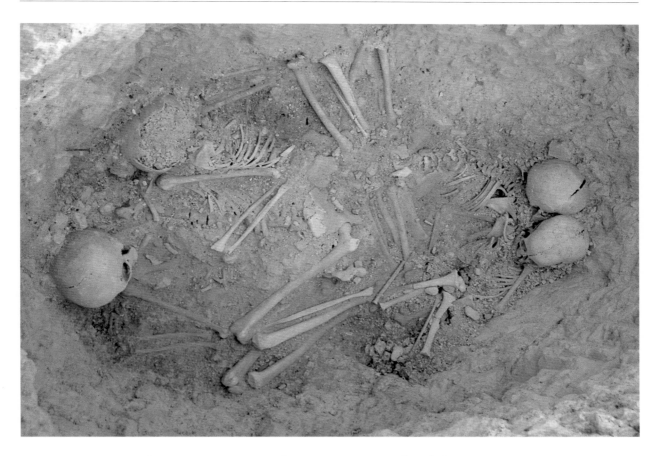

turned into a continuous downpour Martin decided that the fragile bones would suffer from getting too wet. We packed up for the day, covering the grave with a stout construction of planks and tarpaulins weighted down with huge blocks of chalk. The bones would be quite safe under there. That night the heavens opened.

The next morning we found that the whole site had flooded during the night. When Martin pulled back the covers from the grave pit, he was horrified to see it full to the brim with muddy water, small bones bobbing on the surface. There was nothing that Martin could have done to prevent this but, as we baled bucket after bucket of water from the grave we all wondered what state the bones would be in when we finally reached them. As the

The skeletons of a woman and three children, huddled together in death. Were they a family that made the ultimate sacrifice – victims to whatever gods were worshipped nearly 5000 years ago?

bones started to break surface, buckets gave way to spoons and sponges and we realized with relief that most had stayed in place. They were wet and covered in fine sticky silt, but they were undamaged. As the lifting continued, bags were filled with mud the consistency of wet plaster. No matter how carefully the excavation was now carried out, tiny finger and toe bones could easily be lost in the sludge at the bottom of the grave so it all had to be taken back to Jackie's laboratory to be sieved.

It was early autumn by the time the burials were excavated. There was still digging to do, samples to be taken, plans to be drawn, but the end of the excavation was in sight, much to Martin's relief. It had turned out to be a fascinating site, but far more complicated than he could ever have imagined (and the farmer who owned the field was anxious to plough the field and sow his crop). We had all been gripped by what we had seen in the field, but now there were questions to ask, investigations to be carried out. We all wanted to know what story the bones would tell.

There was a certain degree of urgency in Jackie's examination of the bones, particularly those from the burials in the grave which had been flooded. The samples of mud needed to be sieved and the bones cleaned of silt and slowly dried before they could be examined. Adam, much to our relief, indeed turned out to be a man. While he still lay in the ground we had noted the pronounced ridges on the brow of his skull, a very male characteristic, and Jackie could also show us the signs of a male pelvis, narrower than a woman's, and the general robustness of the bones. Adam was between thirty and forty-five when he died, a strongly built man of about 5ft 4in (1.63 metres) in height and showing no signs of how he had died. His bones were in very poor condition, eroded by exposure to roots in their shallow burial under the mound of flints.

In contrast, the bones of the woman from the grave pit were in beautiful condition, preserved by their burial deep in the pure chalk. She was only a little smaller than Adam, a little younger, and, in contrast to his muscular build, was slender and delicately built. Her joints, even at what seems the comparatively young age of thirty, were starting to shows signs of osteoarthritis, and clues to her lifestyle lay in the bones of her lower body. 'Squatting facets' (small changes to her lower limb bones) showed that she had spent considerable periods of time in a crouched position. The most remarkable feature of her beautifully preserved skull was her teeth – a perfect set, neat, regular and showing no signs of decay or disease.

She had shared her grave with three children, perhaps her own, aged about five, eight and nine. There was no way that Jackie could tell whether each burial was of a boy or a girl as the bones of young children have not yet developed the distinguishing features of an adult male or female. None of the children showed any signs of how they had died, although each little skull had small pits in the eye sockets, the telltale signs of iron deficiency. Sadly, the smallest child appeared to have suffered the worst health. Not only did the child have an abscessed tooth but, more disturbingly, Jackie noted signs of tumours in the skull. It is most unusual to find evidence of this type of disease in the bones of one so young, and so the whole skeleton was X-rayed to check for additional tumours. None was found. We tend to think of cancer as a modern disease, a curse of an industrial polluted society, but here we appeared to have evidence of this same disease from a remote time when people lived in harmony with nature.

This was the first stage of finding out about these people but there was so much more that we wanted to know, and even Jackie could not provide all of the answers. The objects found with or close by Adam and the burials in the pit had given us some idea of the date of their burial, but we wanted to know more precisely. The answer lay in radiocarbon dating, a remarkable process which takes any once-living material and dates with some precision the time of its death.

The principle is relatively simple. While they are alive, all living things, whether trees, animals, fish or people, absorb many types of carbon from the atmosphere. These include a radioactive isotope, carbon 14, which, when the living thing dies, starts to lose its radioactivity at a steady and measurable rate. Carbon 14 has a half-life of 5730 years, which means that half of its radioactivity will have disappeared, decayed, in those 5730 years. The amount of decay can be measured against modern control samples and the time that has elapsed since the living thing died can be calculated. This method of dating caused a revolution in the understanding of the prehistoric past when it was first introduced in 1949, and we hoped that it was going to tell us when our people from Cranborne died. One of the great advances in recent years has been a reduction in the amount of bone, wood or charcoal that is needed to provide a date. In its infancy radiocarbon dating often required nearly a whole skeleton to provide sufficient carbon but now, at the Radiocarbon Accelerator in Oxford, tiny samples – only a few grammes – are ground from a bone, usually a dense and solid one such as the femur, leaving the skeleton virtually intact.

Although it is the whole skeleton that provides the clues to sex, age and general health, it is the skull that forms the basis for the face, the part of our bodies which gives us character and individuality. All of us who had seen the skull which belonged to the woman in the grave pit were still fascinated by her perfect teeth. How had someone managed to keep them in such condition thousands of years before toothbrushes were invented? A professional opinion seemed to be required and so we went to Cardiff to see David Whittaker at the University of Wales School of Medicine. David is a specialist in forensic dentistry, used to dealing with more modern teeth than the ones we had brought him, but he too was impressed by our woman's standard of dental health. Her explained that her teeth were not perfect, they were worn, but this was only to be expected when most people's diet would have been much coarser than today's. Apart from the wear, her only problem was with a build-up of tartar on the back of her molars. David thought that to have maintained this envi-

RIGHT: *The Neolithic landscape of Cranborne Chase where the burial of the woman and children was hidden in a strange and maybe disturbing site.*

able standard of dental hygiene would have involved a conscious use of the tongue to continually clean the teeth. This also helps to promote a good flow of saliva and this, in turn, has the effect of inhibiting decay. With a growing mental picture of what this woman may have looked like when she was alive, it was time now to turn to science and see if our imaginations had led us astray.

We took the skull to Robin Richards, who works in the Department of Medical Physics at University College, London. Robin's method of reconstruction for ancient faces has been developed to help in facial reconstruction surgery, but the techniques involved with both ancient and modern skulls are very similar. If the ancient skull is complete then it is mounted on a stand attached to the chair in which live patients sit. A laser beam then maps the contours of the slowly

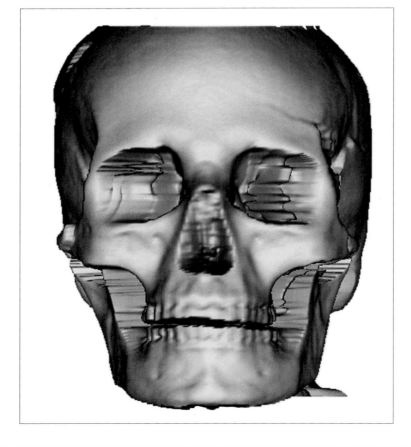

LEFT: *Mapped by laser, the contours of the ancient skull are stored as digitized data that can then be used to generate a computer image, the foundation for the reconstruction of the face.*

RIGHT: *The computer adds the flesh and skin of an average face to the laser mapped skull, creating a mask anatomically correct, but lacking the character of a real face.*

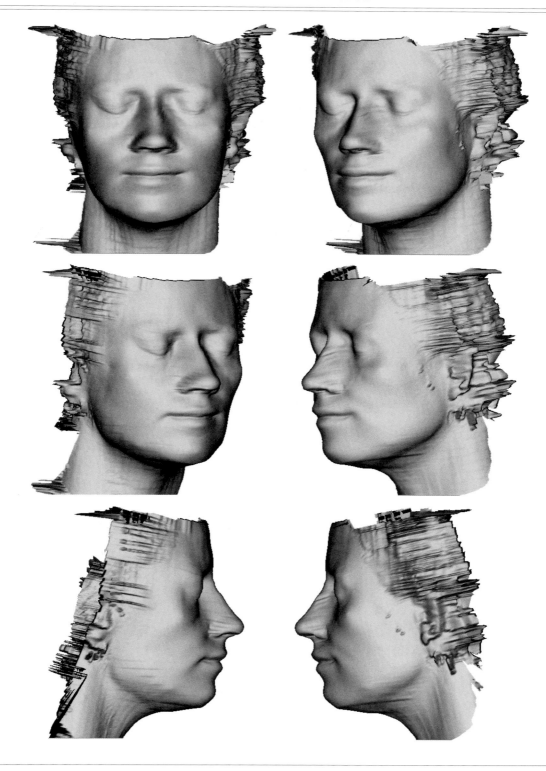

revolving skull, registering thousands of individual points which are recorded by computer. The computer can then produce an image of the skull and, in Robin's surgical work, these data can be used to create a three-dimensional sculptured replica of the skull in rigid foam. For our purposes, what we needed was the flesh to be added back to the skull to create a person from these Neolithic remains. Robin does this by adding to the skull an 'average' face, so what we needed was a face for a slenderly built woman of around thirty years old. 'Averages' are created by scanning the faces of living people of the correct sex and age and letting the computer blend them to iron out any particularly distinctive features. The ancient face is then constructed by identifying the same series of anatomical reference points on both ancient skull and modern face and by merging the two together. Essentially the computer is adding the appropriate skin and tissue depths at each point but the result is far from a human face. What emerges is a smooth computerized mask, with eyes closed and free of the lines and wrinkles which provide character to a real face.

It was now up to our illustrator Jane Brayne to humanize Robin's computer face, to give it life and colour and bring us one step closer to our prehistoric ancestor. This was yet another task for Jane who, since the end of the excavation, had been working on two landscape paintings, showing Martin's strange site at two different times in prehistory. The first was based in Adam's time during the Bronze Age, the second nearly a thousand years earlier in the Neolithic period, the time when the woman and the children in the grave pit had lived. Jane knew when she sketched the modern landscape while the excavation was taking place that the pattern of hills and valleys would not have changed, but she needed to replace the neat hedged fields and the acres of evenly growing corn with something more in keeping. Fortunately, over the years that he has been digging, Martin had managed to persuade Mike Allen, an environmental specialist from Wessex Archaeology, that all of his sites were very interesting. As a result,

RIGHT: *The Bronze Age landscape of Cranborne Chase where Adam's burial took place in the centre of an already ancient site.*

Mike had collected and studied many samples of soils from ditches and pits and from soils buried beneath ancient banks and mounds. Chalk soils are very good for the preservation of bone and they also preserve shells, particularly the tiny snail shells which interest Mike so much. These are the clues to the environment of the past as fortunately snails tend to be very choosy about the habitat they occupy. Some like short grass, others woodland, long grass or broken ground. Sort out the species of snail from the layer underneath a bank and you have the type of environment in which it was constructed.

Mike's interrogation of the tiny ancient snails provided Jane with a clear indication of the nature of the prehistoric landscape, the places where the natural wildwood was cleared and grazing land took over, and where and when this pattern was broken by arable fields. In addition, charred fragments of wood from a variety of excavations showed which species of tree were most common and added to the degree of confidence with which Jane could reconstruct the changing prehistoric landscape.

Adam was buried at a time when the complex monument of central hole, shaft and pits had long been abandoned. Now its only trace was a shallow circular depression, which must have resembled a pond barrow, a peculiar form of 'reversed' or 'negative' round barrow constructed at about this time. Normal round barrows usually have a mound, often surrounded by a ditch, but pond barrows replace this with a circular hollow surrounded by a bank. It was at the centre of this circular depression that Adam's body was placed. Radiocarbon dating suggested that this happened in the middle Bronze Age, around 1500 BC. At this time the landscape is comparatively open, a mosaic of well-grazed grassland interspersed with woods and into which the first real fields and farms are starting to creep. The newly cultivated fields are stony and from here come the large angular flints which pile up to cover and mark Adam's crouched remains. Beyond, on hilltops and in the valleys, newly built round barrows gleam white, brilliant reminders of the newly acquired power of a wealthy few.

Turn the clock back to around 3000 BC and the landscape is closer to its natural state, the mixed 'wildwood' of oak, elm and lime which has blanketed the entire country since the end of the last Ice Age about 12,000 years ago. This woodland is being gradually cleared to provide pasture for the newly introduced domesticated cattle, but also for more spiritual reasons. Through the woodland cuts the great Cursus, a swathe of grassland in which its banks and ditches show stark white. The early farmers who are so busy changing their landscape have invested a huge amount of their precious time and energy building – what? A pathway? We know that at the Winter Solstice, the shortest day of the year and a time of great significance in the pagan calendar, the line of the Cursus acts as an observatory. Face south-west and look down the line of the Cursus from its original end point on Bottlebush Down, and the sun sets directly behind one of the long barrows incorporated into its overall alignment. Martin, who has probably thought more about the Cursus than anyone and who has experienced its magic throughout the changing seasons, gave us the most eloquent and plausible explanation of its meaning. To him it represents 'a place where the earth met the sky and where the mortals that dwelt on the earth could communicate with the gods of the sky'. It was into a landscape already charged with spiritual meaning that Martin's strange site was introduced.

In Jane's illustration (pages 30–31) it is almost completed. In the foreground are the posts, traces of which Martin found in his excavation and which may have served either as a screen or to mark one of the entrances into the site. There is no way of telling what such posts may have looked like – they may have been carved or painted, plain or garlanded with flowers. Perhaps the way in which a Christian church is decorated at Harvest Festival should provide us with a clue. A structure of such scale and complexity must have been a communal effort; perhaps each of the outer pits was the responsibility of a family group, with everyone coming together to dig the great shaft. It is clearly planned, and the planning must have been the responsibility of

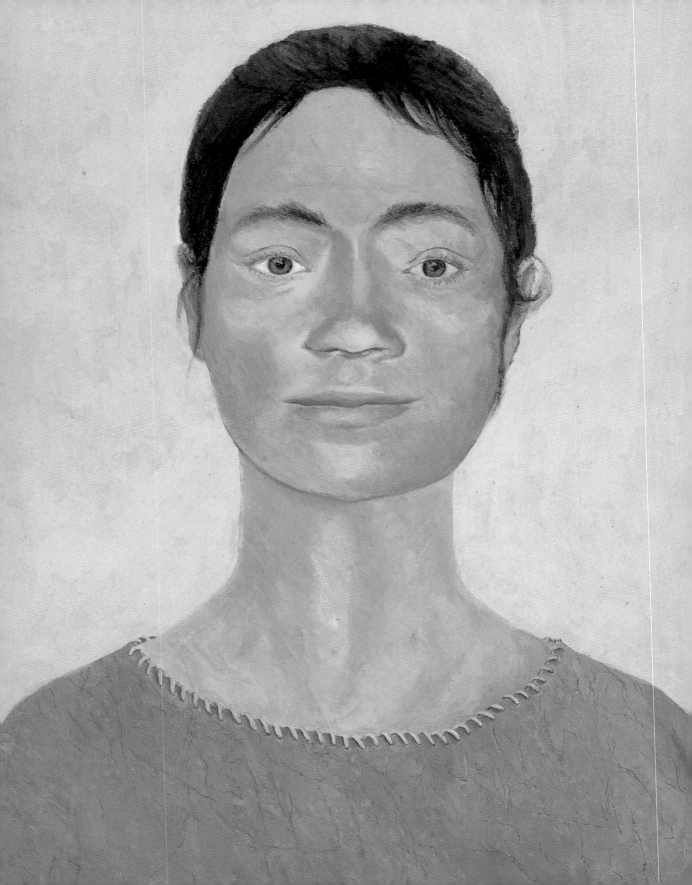

either one individual or a group, someone with the influence and power to motivate. This is the point at which archaeology and science fail to provide the answers. This site was built for a purpose and we can only assume that the purpose was spiritual. Each of its major elements, the pits, the central arena, the shaft, must have had meaning and played its part in ceremonies that we can only guess at. Into this ritually charged site, even before its completion, were placed the burials of four people. Laid in a simple chalk cut pit, the crouched remains of a woman and three small children at first seemed so much like a family overtaken by some unknown tragedy. We know now that the youngest child was perhaps terminally ill, but why did the others die, the older children and the slender young woman with her perfect teeth? There may be a simple reason that their bones cannot tell us, some rapid infection that carried them off together, but perhaps there is a darker reason why they were buried together in their concealed grave. Nearly 5000 years ago the gods may have demanded more than just worship, more than just a chalk temple, carvings and offerings of meat. Perhaps these four, willingly or unwillingly, for the sake of their community and for the blessing of the gods, paid the ultimate sacrifice.

The Neolithic woman from Cranborne Chase, the most ancient of the ancestors that we were able to meet.

BONES IN THE BARNYARD

THE LITTLE VILLAGE of
Bleadon nestles in the shelter of a curving limestone ridge close to the
sea near Weston-super-Mare in Somerset. Its origins are clearly
ancient, the medieval church dominating the village centre, but like
many such villages it is growing rapidly. New houses fill vacant plots
of land, the old vicarage garden has been built over, and a property
developer had his eye on the old yard that belonged to Whitegates
Farm. The farm had been in Anne Ball's family for generations, but
the old barns weren't needed any longer and a site for some new
houses would make better economic sense than the cows.

You cannot build anything without planning permission, though,
and today archaeology is an integral part of the planning process.
North Somerset District Council has its own archaeologist, Vince
Russett, and Vince had a feeling that the old farmyard could lie over
buried remains of the medieval village. So he insisted that the site was

investigated (at the developer's expense) before the planning application was considered. The Avon Archaeological Unit are based in Bristol and carry out a lot of excavations in Somerset. They were given the job of investigating the site, digging trenches with a mechanical digger in between the remains of the barn walls and through the concrete surface of the old yard.

Andy Young, their director, was not really surprised to find medieval remains, just as Vince had predicted. He was surprised by the prehistoric pottery he found and even more surprised when their machine exposed a large circular pit with a human skull sticking out the top of it. By luck or design he had unearthed a prehistoric burial site dating back, so it appeared from the pottery they had found, to around 800 BC, towards the end of the Bronze Age.

This was not just unexpected – it was a very important find as actual burials of bodies which survive as skeletons are quite rare from this time in prehistory. Most of the dead from this time were cremated, either through fashion or religious belief. In the Planning Department Vince had to make up his mind about what should happen to the site, and it all depended on just how important he felt the discoveries were. One option was simply to say no to the building work but, in the end, he decided that it could go ahead though only after a full-scale archaeological excavation of the whole site. Everyone involved chipped in to pay for the work: the developer, the local council and English Heritage who also offered the support of their scientists, specialists in bones, seeds and soils.

As Andy was now going to be able to have more than a tantalizing glimpse of this rare burial site, he contacted *Meet the Ancestors* and invited us to be involved in the next stage of his investigation.

It is often difficult to understand a site from a few small trenches dug with a machine, and as the concrete and rubble were cleared away Andy became aware of just how lucky the positioning of their early trenches had been. More pits appeared, some large, some small, but all clustered around the one which contained the skull, the one which

The graves lay in the centre of the former barn-yard, part of a cluster of unusual historic pits.

had given the first clue to the true nature of the site. After the machines come the human diggers, shovelling and trowelling away the stripped surface, planning and photographing the different soils before any excavation can start. This stage can take what seems an age and we were as eager as Andy and his team to see what was in the pits. Finally it was time to start their investigation.

As work started on the one that we knew contained a skull, we wondered what we would find. Was it just a skull, thrown out with the rubbish, or would the pit turn out to be a grave? As Andrea Cox, one of Andy's team of excavators, gradually removed the soil, the reason for the slightly oval shape of the pit became apparent. It was a grave. The skull, hard up against one edge of the pit and ominously cracked, became part of a complete skeleton, well preserved and lying crouched on its side. The legs were bent and tightly tucked up; one arm was straight down by its side and the other bent up so the fingers lay underneath the chin. Even all the tiny bones of the fingers and toes appeared to be in place. This crouched burial position is common throughout prehistoric times, maybe suggesting someone who is asleep or submissive, or even reflecting the foetal position of a baby in the womb. The skeleton that we could now see fully exposed had lain completely undisturbed just below what was now barnyard concrete for nearly 3000 years.

It is always difficult to say much about a skeleton as it lies in the ground but, as Andrea cleaned around the bones before they were photographed and drawn, all of us had the feeling that this was the burial of a man. It had always been Andy's intention to carry out

DNA analysis on the burials from the site. It is now quite simple to extract DNA from a living person – bits of it fall off us every time we sneeze or scratch our heads – but recent work has managed to extract it from the bones of people who died long ago. What have been extracted are short damaged strands of DNA, certainly not enough to re-create the complete profile of a person from the past, but enough to provide useful information. Great care must be taken in an excavation not to contaminate old specimens with modern DNA, and this meant digging in rubber surgical gloves – a very unpleasant experience, especially on a warm day. As the final cleaning was carried out we could see that the man had nothing in his grave to tell us when he had been buried apart from the fragments of pottery which lay by his feet. Were these and his bones going to provide enough clues for us to re-create a prehistoric life?

A few metres away lay another pit which appeared at first to be packed with small rocks. Under these lay another skeleton, this time of a woman, but badly crushed

The skeleton of a woman lay in another pit, crushed by the weight of stones that had been piled up to mark her grave.

by the weight of rock that had been placed over her to mark the grave. Crushed though her bones were, this burial provided the first clue that not everything on the excavation might be as old as the Bronze Age. Under her chin lay a small circular loop of corroded metal, the sort of object that would not be given a second glance if it lay in a field. But here in the grave it became much more important. As it was lifted out we realized that whatever the original form of the object, it was not made of bronze – it was iron. Not surprisingly, iron was first introduced only in the Iron Age which comes straight after the Bronze Age. The first burial, though, had Bronze Age pottery in the grave. Like most sites, rather than becoming simpler as the excavation progressed, it was becoming more and more of a puzzle.

The burials, fascinating and confusing, were only part of the site that was now being excavated. There were more pits, some huge and floored with slabs of limestone, some containing fragments of human bone among the more normal debris of animal bone, pottery and charcoal that seemed to suggest that people were living very close by. Andy had realized when he dug his first exploratory trenches that the site had great potential to provide valuable clues about prehistoric life as well as death. Were these people farmers? What crops and animals did they have? What were their surroundings like? Would they still recognize Bleadon if they came back 3000 years after they died? Andy knew that the clues which could help to answer these questions would be very subtle; experts would be needed to take away samples of soil and to advise on how the site should be excavated. They started to arrive as the excavation swung into top gear.

Richard McPhail came down from University College, London, to look at the soils on the site and in the nearby fields. He was sure that their structure would tell him about changes in prehistoric vegetation, the way that people had altered the natural environment in their search for food, shelter and warmth. Hammering an open-sided metal box into the edge of the excavation trench, Richard could capture a slice through time. In his box were all the layers of soil which had built up over the undisturbed natural bedrock, from before our pre-historic people arrived on site to the time of the modern farm. But what about the surrounding landscape? We had already noticed that traces of small square fields, defined by low banks and stone walls, lay on the hill slopes above the excavation site. These ancient fields showed where the crops were once grown, but what about the flat, low-lying fields below the site? Today they are dry, with drainage ditches surrounding them on all sides, although we were told that they do still occasionally flood. But what were they like 3000 years ago? Maybe this low-lying area had been marshy, with stagnant pools and tangled vegetation of willows and alders, a place for hunting and gathering wood, but of little use to a farmer. If this was the case then peat, the remains of waterlogged vegetation, might lie beneath the surface, peat with the potential for answering all sorts of environmental questions. There was only one way to find out – to have a look – but it was felt that the farmer might not take too kindly to large machine-dug trenches in his best grass field.

The problem was solved by Matt Canti from English Heritage's Ancient Monuments Laboratory who arrived in a Transit van with a load of scaffolding poles, some hollow probes and a pneumatic drill. Drilling the probes in was no problem – though levering them out again was a different matter – but the results were worth the effort. There were no thick bands of peat to indicate a swampy environment, just fine clays laid down by many episodes of flooding, interleaved with occasional thin bands of peat. What this showed immediately was that in prehistoric times this area had been a salt marsh, providing seasonal grazing, vital to the success of the farming economy.

Richard can usually find what he needs in one visit, taking his bit of the site back to a warm laboratory for study. The clues that another English Heritage consultant, Vanessa Straker from Bristol University, was seeking lay within the tons of soil which filled the deep pits and which first had to be extracted. If the people who lived here in prehistoric times had been farmers then these soils should contain traces of

Searching for environmental clues using a power auger to collect samples of soil from the fields below the site.

their crops, seeds and chaff, fragile remains that unless waterlogged will generally survive only when charred by fire. Fortunately, a few often do get charred, either as part of a drying process or simply by ending up too close to a fire. There is only one way to recover these remains: by 'flotation', a process involving sieving in a stream of running water. One of the least favourite tasks on any site is sieving. This is hardly surprising as it is not only tedious but involves standing ankle deep in mud by a Heath Robinson contraption made from an old oil drum, a few bits of sheet metal and piping, with a hosepipe in your hand and water running down your boots. It's not too bad in summer but when the weather is cold it's miserable. Everyone on site took turns as soil turned to mud and the charred fragments floated over the lip of the tank to be caught in the fine sieve below. At first it all seemed like charcoal but then seeds started to appear, just the odd one to start with, but then more and more, and the discomfort suddenly all seemed worth while.

We suddenly realized that the clues were here on site, and the answers to all our questions lay in Richard's blocks of soil and Vanessa's little charred seeds, in the animal bones that were being dug from the pits and collected in the sieves. If Jane Brayne, our illustrator, was going to bring all these strands together and reconstruct the prehistoric landscape, we needed a framework, a view of today's landscape, and where better to see this than from the top of the church tower. The spiral stone stairs that led upwards seemed endless, but the view when we finally arrived was wonderful. The excavation site was clearly visible and we realized with some dismay that it was surrounded on nearly all sides by recent housing. How much vital information had been destroyed without record before archaeology finally became a part of the whole planning process in the 1980s?

The man's skeleton lay tightly crouched in the burial pit, his head bent up against its side. Perhaps this position symbolized sleep to those who buried him.

What was most obvious from our vantage point were the reasons
for the position of the village. It lies at the base of a low limestone
ridge, the gently curving arms of which seem to enfold and offer
shelter and protection. We had already noticed the ancient fields
immediately below the crest of the ridge, above the village, but from
the church tower it was obvious that they had originally been far more
extensive. Running out from the surviving fragments of ancient
fields, long boundaries continue their lines, running down slopes
until some become fossilized in the bound-
aries between village properties. I wondered
if the people who lived in these cottages
knew that their garden wall still followed

*The least favourite job on site
– wet-sieving soil to retrieve
animal bones and seeds.*

a boundary laid out thousands of years ago by a prehistoric farmer, maybe one of their ancestors.

It was also clear that whoever chose this spot for a settlement didn't want to get their feet wet. Quite sensibly, the extent of the houses, both old and new, reflects the boundary between dry land and that still prone to flood. Beyond the flat fields, which we had discovered were salt marsh, lies the sea, less than two miles away, perhaps an extra source of food for our ancient coastal community.

The excavation caused enormous interest in Bleadon and the surrounding villages. Vince and Andy gave guided tours of the site and stressed to those who came on them that it was important to view the burials as the remains of people not just as archaeological specimens. The *Weston and Somerset Mercury* provided weekly dig reports and the board outside the village shop proclaimed 'Bronze Age Dig – latest news'. Odd things continued to be discovered, like the animal burials which appeared close to the edge of the excavation trench, some distance away from the burial pits. In a shallow scoop in the soil lay the complete skeletons of what appeared to be two dogs and immediately our imaginations ran riot. Were these favourite hunting dogs belonging to the man in the pit, sacrificed and buried at the time of his death? It made a good story but not good enough for the paper; by the time they got hold of it the dogs had become wolves.

Finally, after four weeks, the excavation was finished. The bones from the graves had been carefully lifted and packaged away, the pits were empty and the last bucket of soil had been sieved. It was time for Andy and his team to reflect on a job well done, on a site that had already sprung some surprises and that would spring some more before the work of analysing the finds was complete.

It is quite tempting to relax once an excavation is over, although this is difficult if you run a busy archaeological organization as Andy does. You might think that once all the finds are boxed up and the site records neatly filed away that this would be the time for a rest, but there are some things that cannot wait. Iron is one of them. The iron object from the woman's grave had lain in the soil for at least 2000 years and during that time had reached a state of equilibrium, corroded but stable – the process of decay had effectively stopped. Dig it up and expose it to the air and the processes of corrosion start all over again.

This meant that the iron object had to be looked at very quickly before vital information was lost or it disintegrated entirely. Metal objects when excavated may be totally unrecognizable under a thick crust of corrosion, so Meg Brooks's first task at the Conservation Laboratory in Salisbury was to X-ray all those rescued from the site. As well as the original form of an object, X-rays can also show details of manufacture – the multiple strands of metal that are forged into a single iron blade, or the use of different metals such as tin-plating applied to iron. It was the object from the grave that we were interested in, though, and the X-rays showed clearly that it was a brooch, almost completely round in shape and with the remnants of a pin surviving. Mark Corney, our Iron Age (and Roman) expert from Bristol University, knew exactly what it was, a 'penannular' or nearly circular brooch, and he was also sure that it could not date to much earlier than about 200 BC. It certainly wasn't Bronze Age.

This was the first clue that the burials, or at least one of them, weren't quite as early as Vince and Andy had expected. But this just whetted our appetite to find out more about the two people who had been buried in Bleadon at least 2000 years ago. We were reunited with their bones at Simon Mays's laboratory at the English Heritage HQ in London. Having only seen the skeletons crouched in small pits in the ground, it was quite a surprise to see them laid out with all their bones in the correct order. But not all intact. There had been a disaster with the man's skull. In the ground it had seemed merely cracked, yet now we had not a complete skull but over a hundred fragments. The likelihood of being able to reconstruct it and rebuild the man's face suddenly seemed quite remote. This seemed a tremendous blow, but Simon was confident that it could be done and, after

all, he had seen a lot more bones than we had. As we tried not to think about this potential problem, Simon explained what he had been able to find from the bones and the fascination of emerging lives took over.

The excavation site lay in the centre of Bleadon village, viewed here from the top of the church tower.

We had got the sexes correct. The rather crushed burial with the iron brooch was of a woman and the other, with the now fragmented skull, was of a man, about 5ft 6in (1.68 metres) tall according to the calculations Simon made from the length of his thigh bones. The wear on his teeth suggested that he was about fifty years old when he died and, although his lower jaw showed clear signs of severe abscesses, it was strong. Simon explained that this strength, which would have given our man a firm, 'lantern' jawline, is typical of people up to relatively recent times who were used to a much coarser diet than we eat today. Roughly ground flour, root vegetables and meat that was probably very tough by our standards are very different to the soft processed foods that we tend to eat today and which require very little chewing. As Simon succinctly put it, many of us today eat 'factory-made pap'. Although Bleadon Man may have eaten a healthy diet and had an enviably masculine jawline, I was glad that I did not have to suffer the agonies of toothache that he must have endured. There are certain advantages to living in the twentieth century and dental care is most definitely one of them.

Simon had also found some good indications of the stature and strength of Bleadon Man. The bones of the body provide a framework on to which muscles are attached. Large, robust bones tend to mean a person with a strong build, and the more pronounced the place where the muscles are attached, the stronger those muscles are likely to be. To judge from the size of his bones and the pronounced nature of his muscle attachments, Bleadon Man was a strongly built individual. Perhaps his strength came from hard manual labour in the fields — possibly the reason why his hip joints were starting to show the tell-tale signs of wear which go with quite severe arthritis. A picture was starting to emerge of a person, perhaps a farmer, but there were still so many questions unanswered. When did he die? Were any of the villagers from Bleadon who had gazed at him as he lay in his grave his distant relatives? What had he looked like?

We hoped that the answers to the first two questions lay in the tiny samples of thigh bone which Simon removed. One would go to Oxford for radiocarbon dating, the other to DNA expert Erica Hegelberg in Cambridge. Her first task was to see if DNA still survived in the bone and, if so, whether it could be successfully extracted. DNA is a remarkable substance which carries the instructions needed to build a body, whether a chimpanzee or a human. Its full name is deoxyribonucleic acid, and its extraction from a living person is very easy, all that is needed is a small sample of hair, saliva or blood. Recent work has managed to extract short damaged pieces of DNA from the bones of people who died long ago, not enough to re-create the complete profile of a person from the past, but enough to provide Erica with the information that she needed. Erica explained to us that the process she needed to follow was complex and that great care had to be taken not to contaminate the ancient samples with modern DNA. Ideally, bones should only be handled wearing rubber gloves and face masks help prevent contamination from coughs and sneezes. If we could obtain DNA from an ancient inhabitant of Bleadon then we would need to compare it with samples from today's population.

For the answer to the third question we needed to see Richard Neave at the University of Manchester Medical School. Richard is one of the country's leading experts in facial reconstruction, and often has the harrowing but ultimately rewarding task of identifying missing people or victims of crime from their often fragmentary remains. His numerous successes in this area have lead to collaboration with archaeologists in the reconstruction of such famous individuals as Philip II of Macedonia and Lindow Man (often known as 'Pete Marsh'), Britain's most famous bog body.

Much to our relief, Richard was totally unconcerned by the state of the skull we presented him with. Over two days, using a special sticky wax and numerous tiny wooden pegs as supports, the skull regained its original form. As he worked, Richard explained how the skull determines the character of the face. Its basic proportions come from the overall shape of the skull, the distance between the eyes, the depth of the upper jaw, the angle of the nose. But the skull is more than just the foundation: in it lie the clues that give each of us our individuality. Richard also showed us how the shape of the eye socket could determine whether eyes were level, or turned up or down, how the shape of the lower jaw could indicate a cleft chin, how the nasal bone gave clues not only to the angle but also the shape of the nose.

Finally the skull was complete and the process of building a face could begin – not on the real skull, though. This was still an important part of the archaeological record of the site and everything that had happened to it so far could be easily reversed. This would not be the case once the face building started so, after the last few missing bits of bone were replaced with wax, an accurate cast was made in

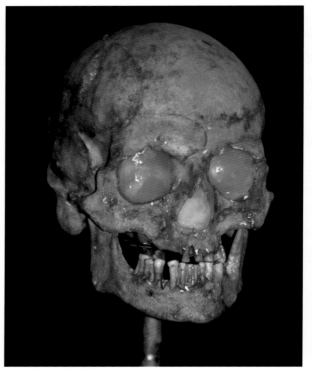

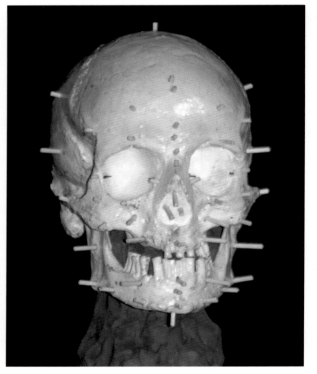

1 The skull of Bleadon Man was painstakingly
reconstructed from more than a hundred fragments.
The eye and nose sockets are filled with wax prior to
a cast being made. The overall shape of the skull
determines the basic proportions of the face.

2 Plaster cast of the skull with the twenty pegs,
placed at precise locations, that mark the final
depth of muscles, soft tissue and skin. The
length of the pegs at these points is carefully
calculated from a series of tables.

plaster. It was then very obvious why the real skull could not be used,
as the next stage involved Caroline Wilkinson, one of Richard's medical artists, drilling twenty small holes into the cast at precisely deter-
mined locations. Into each of these holes a thin wooden peg is
inserted, and cut off to leave a precisely calculated length sticking
out. How much protrudes is worked out from a series of tables giving
the depths of muscle and soft tissue at each of these points, so the end
of the pegs will eventually mark the surface of the skin on the completed face. For Bleadon Man we knew that he was male, aged about
fifty and of strong build, all factors which are built into the calcula-

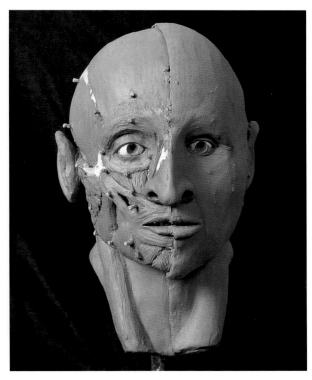

Strips of clay are laid over the skull in strict anotomical order. As successive layers of muscles and tissue are applied, the final shape of the face starts to form. Bleadon Man's prominent nose first became apparent at this stage.

tion of peg depth. It was at this point that the reconstruction started to look like something from a horror film, made even worse when the plaster eyeballs were inserted. The muscles which form the next layer are made of strips of clay; and watching Caroline applying them, in strict anatomical order, brought home to us how complicated our faces are. They are so mobile, capable not only of carrying out functions like chewing but of expressing a huge range of emotions. As a particular muscle was applied to the plaster skull we would all find ourselves twitching and grimacing, attempting to find out exactly what it did in our faces. As layers of muscles and tissue were applied in a very sculptural way, the face gradually took shape. It became very obvious that one of Bleadon Man's most distinctive features was his nose. Put quite bluntly, it was a whopper and would remain so even as the rest of the face was built up around it.

As Caroline carried on with Bleadon Man's face we heard that Erica had managed to extract ancient DNA from his bones. The success of this process was not a foregone conclusion, as there are many factors which can affect the survival of ancient DNA. Now we needed the samples from the villagers if we were to demonstrate a link between prehistory and the present day. It was clearly no use testing all of the people who lived in the village as some of them may only have moved there quite recently from the other side of the country. What we needed were families who had lived there for generations, families that we could identify by looking back through the parish records. We soon found thirteen family names, including Amesbury, Fear, Priston, Spurlock and Young, and contacted them with our odd request for a little bit of their blood in the cause of science. The response was very encouraging, so Coronation Hall in the middle of the village was taken over, nurses brought in and, amid a lot of light-hearted speculation about who might have this particular prehistoric ancestor, the samples were taken. Erica went back to work.

Returning to Bleadon, where the houses were now going up on the old excavation site, reawakened our curiosity about what the village had looked like in prehistoric times. Some of the answers were provided by those blocks of soil that Richard McPhail had taken back to his laboratory. Richard had first impregnated them with resin that left the blocks as solid as rock once it had hardened. They could then be cut into thin slices which, under the microscope, revealed in the arrangement of soil particles that the pits at Bleadon were dug in an area not long cleared from woodland. We already knew about the salt marsh in the low-lying fields below the site, and a picture of the landscape was beginning to form in our minds. As yet it was devoid of animals and crops but, if our man really had been a farmer, then he would surely have needed both?

Dale Sergeantson is an English Heritage animal-bone specialist based at Southampton University, where a huge bone reference collection covering everything from frogs to ferrets is housed. Dale's first rapid scan of the bones as they lay spread out on her benches identified lots of sheep, a few cattle, some horse and dog but, surprisingly, no pigs. The sheep were not the large creatures that we are familiar with today but small goat-like animals with shaggy wool, most like the modern Soay sheep. Embarrassingly, the 'ritual' double dog burial (or wolf burial if you read the local paper) turned out to be a pair of sheep, and not even very old ones as Dale pointed out by comparing the size of the bones with some genuine old ones. The cattle too were surprisingly small, something that Dale was able to demonstrate when she took us to the Cotswold Countryside Park. Here they have not only Soay sheep but also Dexters, the nearest equivalent of prehistoric cattle. We all found it hard to

Soays, the small goat-like modern equivalent of Iron Age sheep.

believe that these tiny black cows, no more than a metre high at the shoulder, could not only have provided milk but also have been used as plough animals. It was a shame that Dale hadn't found any pig bones, as we could only glance briefly at the Park's prehistoric pigs, wonderful creatures bred by crossing a wild boar with a domestic pig and which now produce very lively stripy piglets.

The cattle and sheep at Bleadon were obviously used for their meat as well as for milk and wool, as butchery marks made on the bones showed very clearly. Dale also found horse bones which had the same sort of marks, showing that they too were eaten. What was curious about the horses, though, was the way in which their skulls were used. Some were buried in pits, but showing clear evidence that this had happened only after they had been out in the open for quite some time, long enough for teeth to drop out and be lost. Did this suggest that horse skulls were used in some sort of ritual, perhaps associated with the burials that were taking place in other pits?

To Dale the collection of bones from the excavation was typically Iron Age, and exactly what would be left by ancient farmers who wasted nothing. Cows, sheep and horses were all eaten, not only their meat but the nutritious marrow which could be extracted from their cracked bones. There was one puzzle, though. While the sieving of all those tons of soil which Andy's team carried out had produced lots of small bones, many of which would have not been spotted even by the most careful digger, Dale found it odd that they included very few fish bones. Why, on a site which lay so close to the sea, did fish not appear to have been a significant part of the diet? Maybe the answer lay in the crops?

For Vanessa, the sieving had certainly paid off with a fine collection of charred seeds. From these she was able to suggest that the prehistoric farmers, among whom we now included our man, would have grown two different types of ancient wheat, spelt and emmer, as well as barley and oats. Without prompting, Vanessa also expressed her opinion that what she had seen through her microscope looked more like typical Iron Age crops than anything from the Bronze Age. The evidence for a later date seemed to be mounting.

Whatever the actual date of the burials, which was soon going to be resolved by the radiocarbon dates, it seemed as if Jane had enough

information to start work on her reconstruction of the prehistoric landscape. Before she started it seemed like a good idea to bring together everyone who had been involved in the excavation and the subsequent analysis. This was quite a lively session where differences of opinion were aired and the question of the site's date was raised yet again. Finally some consensus of opinion was reached about the setting of the site (if not its date) and Jane went back to her studio to translate her sketches and notes into a finished picture. The form of the landscape, drawn from the vantage point on the church tower, could now be cloaked in vegetation, the ancient fields on the hill slopes could be brought back to life, and prehistoric people and their animals could populate what was, many years later, to become the village of Bleadon. The question of exactly where the people who were buried on the site had lived was still unanswered. We all felt that it must have been close by, perhaps where the centre of the

Bleadon in the late Iron Age. Farmers cultivate the fertile slopes and animals graze the rich meadows, with ceremony and burial reserved for a small woodland clearing close to the salt marsh edge.

modern village now lies, and so Jane, with everyone's agreement, showed a cluster of round huts lying within a fenced enclosure – the sort of place that our man from Bleadon would have recognized as home.

With his home and surroundings reconstructed, at least on paper, it was now time to meet the completed Bleadon Man. The last time I had seen the head it had resembled an anatomical model, a skull clad in muscles, lacking ears and with a nose that seemed huge and beak-like. Now with the soft tissue complete, with ears, hair and a stubbly beard, I met a person, a strong-looking individual with an air of hardship about him, a more rugged face than the one that I had expected. In creating a face Richard and his team start with their knowledge of anatomy, but it is Richard's unique understanding of the way a human face ages that gives humanity to his creations. He always says that the faces make themselves, that he cannot influence the way they eventually turn out, and that he feels that anyone who knew the person in life would recognize them from his finished face.

As the final pieces of the jigsaw started to slot into place there were still unanswered questions. Did our man live and die in the Bronze Age or the Iron Age? At last we found out at the Oxford Radiocarbon Accelerator where Chris Ramsey gave me the results of the dating that had been carried out on part of our man's thigh bone. He was Iron Age. Both he and the woman who lay close by had been buried some time between 200 and 100 BC, at least 500 years after the end of the Bronze Age. The pottery which came from the man's grave, and which first suggested when he was buried, must have been lying around on the site for hundreds of years. Now the radiocarbon dates could confirm that the suspicions raised by the iron brooch and the hints from the seeds and animal bones had been correct. The dates were quite enough to make our trip to Oxford worth while but there was an added bonus from the analysis that had been carried out there. At the same time as the dating is carried out, stable isotopes from the bone are analysed and can provide an indication of diet. Marine and land plants contain different ratios of the carbon isotopes 12C and 13C. As these plants are eaten by animals the different ratios are passed on down the food chain until they can end up fixed in human bones. Here they can provide an indication of whether much of the protein in a person's diet was derived from marine or land-based food sources. The isotopes from the bones of Bleadon Man confirmed what the animal bones from the site had hinted at: the man's diet, despite him living so close to the sea, didn't include fish. He was a farmer, not a fisherman.

As a farmer, it could reasonably be expected that he would have some descendants among Bleadon's present-day farming community. But the results of Erica's DNA analysis were even more surprising than we had expected. Of the forty-eight villagers who gave blood samples, Erica had been able to extract DNA from all of them and within this group there were five whose DNA sequence had marked similarities with that of Bleadon Man. Erica would be the first to admit that the evidence would not allow her to say that these five were direct descendants of our man, but there was certainly a link and we wanted to introduce them to one of their possible ancestors. It seemed like a good idea to include the whole village and take the opportunity to update everyone on what had been happening since Andy's team left the site, so, once again, we commandeered the Coronation Hall for a Saturday afternoon.

The place was packed as Andy, Jane, Erica and I explained the work we had been busy with over the previous six months. Then came the time to unveil the face that Richard Neave had rebuilt for us. The reaction from the villagers was instantaneous and unanimous: there was only one person in the village that it could be. They were right. As we called out the names of the famous five whose DNA matched and presented each of them with a commemorative certificate, we knew who the villagers were talking about. Not David Durston, not Raymond Bailey, not Margaret James or Doris Gould who thought Bleadon Man looked a 'bit miserable'. It was Guy Gibbs who bore

such a striking resemblance to the face that Richard and Caroline had created that it was quite unnerving to see them pose together. Their lives were spent in the same village, even if they were over 2000 years apart, but from their faces they could have been brothers.

It was good to be back in Bleadon for this remarkable end to a fascinating story. Here we had found an Iron Age farmer, whose life was tied up with the land. Around him, in life and in death, lay his fields and grazing land, his crops and animals, an ordered landscape that he helped to create. It is the legacy of his efforts which still helps to define the character of the Somerset countryside to this day.

LEFT: *The rugged face of Bleadon Man, rebuilt from the shattered fragments of an Iron Age skull that lay for centuries beneath the barnyard of Whitegates Farm.*

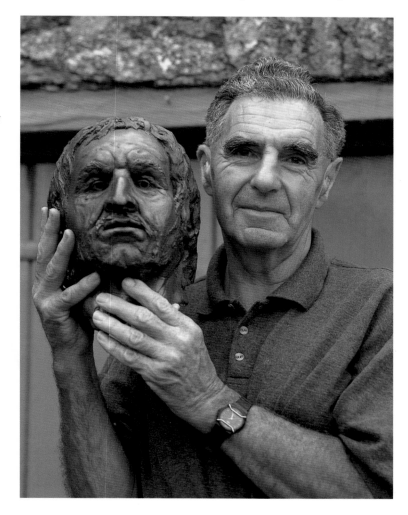

RIGHT: *Bleadon Man with Guy Gibbs, one of his descendants. The similarity was both striking and unexpected.*

FRIENDS, ROMANS OR COUNTRYMEN?

UNTIL QUITE RECENTLY Mangotsfield was a small village on the outskirts of Bristol but, over the last few years, it seems as if the city has come out to meet it. Fields and farms, lanes and woods have gradually disappeared under houses and shops as the city continues to expand. Even Mangotsfield school was not safe from the encroaching development and, when it eventually grew too small to take the children from the new houses, it closed and its grounds were sold for housing.

None of the generations of schoolchildren who had played on its sports field could have had any idea of what lay just a few centimetres below their feet. Neither had Andy Young of the Avon Archaeological Unit when he was called in to investigate the site. He did know that finds of Roman date had been made in the fields surrounding the school and that this had alerted the archaeologist in the local planning department. Over the last few years changes in planning regulations have meant that sites which are proposed for building or any other type of development are investigated if there is any chance that they conceal buried archaeological remains. This was why the developers had been asked to have their site investigated, and at their expense.

The first trenches that Andy's team dug revealed traces of filled-in ditches and scatters of broken pottery, stone and tile. The ditches were the markers for ancient fields, their pattern bearing no resemblance to the familiar layout created by the lanes and hedges that were just about to be swept away. The clue to the date of these ancient fields lay in the scraps of pottery: they were Roman. There were also tantalizing hints in the stone and tiles that somewhere, quite close by, lay a substantial Roman building, but not within the trenches that they were digging. But then, with a clang, the bucket of their mechanical digger hit something large and unyielding. Was this the building that they had hoped for? At first the block of limestone looked solid, and Andy and his diggers assumed that it must be part of a wall. As more soil was cleared away, though, what finally appeared was a long stone box complete with a cracked lid. Andy realized that what they had found was a stone coffin.

This was totally unexpected and was greeted by Andy and the developers in slightly differing ways. As an archaeologist, Andy was excited and curious about what it might hold, while the developers were worried about the implications for their housebuilding. It was clearly an important find, though, and it was eventually decided that the whole area of the housing development would now need to be fully excavated. This could not happen immediately so the coffin was carefully covered over and plans were drawn up for a more extensive digging campaign. We had already worked with Andy at Bleadon, and he knew that we would not be able to resist this new find. So when he returned to strip the turf and topsoil from a much larger area, we went along too.

The school site was easy to find – the gates were still there – but beyond these lay only piles of rubble and the concrete bases where classrooms had once stood. Picking our way through the rubble in the Land Rover, we could see the playing fields, the once immaculate turf now overgrown and scarred by Andy's backfilled trenches. The trench that had first revealed the coffin had not shown any other burials, but did this mean that it lay in splendid isolation in the middle of a Roman field? Roman regulations forbade burial inside any type of settlement, town or village, but normally burials would be expected to cluster together in cemeteries, some small, some very large. As the area around the coffin was stripped and scraped clean, eyes were peeled for signs of further graves, but none appeared and the mystery deepened.

Mark Corney, our Roman expert, works just down the road at Bristol University, and it was very easy to persuade him to come and have a look at the coffin when it was once again revealed. He was certain that it was Roman in date and, although basically a coffin, would have been referred to as a 'sarcophagus', a term which originally meant 'flesh-consuming stone'. The direction in which it lay gave clues about the beliefs of its occupant. Had he or she been a Christian then the sarcophagus would almost certainly have been aligned east–west. In fact it lay northeast–southwest and Mark felt that whoever lay inside it was probably a pagan, a believer not in one God but in the great variety of Roman and Celtic gods.

Andy now faced a real dilemma. The soils on the site lay over a mixture of clay and coal measures and were sufficiently acidic to have destroyed bone over the centuries. But the sarcophagus was made of limestone and bones buried in limestone soils tend to be well preserved. Within this lidded box could be a very well-preserved skeleton, so should he try to remove the sarcophagus from the site complete with its contents or excavate them where it lay? It is an archaeologist's responsibility to ensure the safety of any remains that they are investigating, and Andy was very worried that he could not guarantee this on such an unprotected site. In the end he decided, despite the problems that he knew it would entail, that the sarcopha-

Andy Young's unexpected find: a Roman sarcophagus complete with lid.

LEFT: *Everyday pottery from Roman times. The tall, 'dimpled' vessels were for drinking, the jars and bowls for the storage, preparation and cooking of food.*

gus had to be lifted complete and taken to the museum in Bristol where it could be excavated in security and comfort.

Lifting large and fragile objects estimated to weigh in at over 1 tonne is not part of an archaeologist's normal daily work and Andy, very sensibly, decided to get some professional help. Back at Bristol University he found someone who was willing to take up the challenge. Adam Crewe is a civil engineer and he decided that the answer lay in something very simple and very strong. The design he pencilled out was for a lifting cradle, basically four lengths of very strong 'T' section steel, simply bolted together and suspended at each corner by massive lifting eyes. You cannot get a steel cradle for a coffin off the shelf and so, while one was being built, Andy got on with the excavation of the rest of the site.

The field ditches continued to produce evidence of Roman life over 1500 years ago, and we watched in fascination for any clues about the life of whoever lay in the sarcophagus. Some things, like fragments of pottery, were obviously regarded as rubbish and had been thrown away. Some of the objects had clearly been lost: coins, brooches and a folding knife, the iron blade corroded away to nothing but with a beautiful bronze handle, decorated with a dog chasing a hare. It was easy to imagine the owner's distress at losing such a favourite possession. More fragments of clay tiles appeared, some decorated with patterns of wavy lines. Not decoration, explained Mark Corney, but something for plaster to grip on to. What looked like tiles were pieces of hollow square bricks, flue tiles which took hot air up inside a wall from an underfloor heating system. These fragments of flue brick were more proof that the elusive building lay very close at hand. A building with heating seemed to imply someone wealthy, and some of the fragments of pottery from the ditches seemed to back up this idea. There were cooking pots and pie dishes, blackened with soot from the fire, some locally made, others from Dorset. A fragment of pale pottery with grit pressed into the clay turned out to be part of a 'mortarium', a shallow spouted bowl for grinding and mixing food.

But alongside these ordinary household pots were fine red table wares from Gaul and amphorae from Spain, not imported as empty vessels but filled with either wine or olive oil. Were the people who lived here Romans? Maybe the answer lay in the sarcophagus.

The components of Adam's cradle finally arrived on site and it was time for some heavy work. When it was originally buried the sarcophagus had been lowered down into a grave barely large enough to take it. Lifting it out of this grave was going to be impossible – there was no room to fit the cradle in – so the grave had to be enlarged. Digging through solid bedrock with a pick and shovel was obviously not the most popular job on site but, as no archaeological damage could be caused, it was ideal for members of the film crew. As the grave was enlarged into a substantial pit more of the sides of the sarcophagus were revealed and at first all seemed well. However, in order to insert the cradle we had to undermine the lower edges of the sarcophagus, leaving it perched on a narrow ridge of undisturbed bedrock. As we started the undermining, disaster struck. Cracks suddenly appeared and rapidly widened. One complete corner of the sarcophagus threatened to fall off completely. Emergency measures were clearly called for and, after much rushing around and mild panic, wide straps were obtained and cranked up so tight that there was no possibility of further movement.

It was now very obvious that the extra weight of the lid was not helping matters and it was decided that it had to come off. As the lid was removed we could see immediately that the sarcophagus was completely full of soil that must have trickled and washed in between the cracked fragments. Andy decided that it would be wise to reduce the weight of the soil, the cause of at least some of the problems, and much to everyone's excitement, bones soon appeared. The top of a skull appeared close to the surface at the wider end of the sarcophagus and we had the proof that it was occupied after all. Andy's decision to lift it intact had been the right one all along. Finally it was all strapped together and the cradle, which seemed to weigh almost as much as the sarcophagus itself, was bolted into place. As the massive frame was tightened up it certainly seemed to help pull the cracked stone together. The anxious moments were not yet over, though — there was still the lift to come.

On the day of the lift the excavation came to a standstill as representatives from the museum, the local press and the developers gathered with the excavation team to witness the event. Adam was there too, confident, as a civil engineer should be, that his design would work. But there was always the potential for another, even greater, disaster than the previous day's near collapse. No one had yet seen the base of the sarcophagus; was it as badly cracked as the sides? In fact we didn't know if it had one. Would the lift be accompanied by the bottom falling out of the sarcophagus, leaving its contents in a heap in the bottom of the grave? The suspense was almost too much to bear.

After all the preparation the actual lift seemed to happen very quickly. The four-wheel-drive crane truck swung on to site and carefully picked its way through the numerous sections of open Roman ditch which now pitted the excavated area. The chains were attached to the lifting eyes and the crane began to take the strain. As the gauge registered 1.1 tonnes the cradle and its contents swung into the air. Everyone gathered around instinctively bent down to peer underneath and to our delight we could see that the sarcophagus appeared to have an intact base. As the cradle settled on to the bed of the lorry and was lashed down ready for its journey Adam wore an expression of satisfaction and Andy's relief was obvious. The reason that it had all gone so well lay in the planning. They had both done a splendid job and now it was time for the next stage of the investigation.

After centuries in rural isolation the sarcophagus and its occupant came to town. Andy's choice of the museum warehouse, part of the old Bristol docks, as the destination for the sarcophagus was dictated by one major consideration. Wherever it was going needed to have a very strong

Anxious moments as the crane took the strain and the sarcophagus inched into the air.

*In the museum warehouse the sarcophagus was
gently lowered on to a sturdy stand, ready for
the next stage of the investigation.*

floor. Andy Clarke, one of the team on site, had been chosen to excavate the coffin and he reckoned that the location was ideal. In the
warehouse he would have no problems with the weather, the lighting
was good and it was only a minute's walk from a sandwich bar.
Having already had a quick peek at a skull at the wider end of the sarcophagus, just where you would expect it to be, it seemed perfectly
logical to Andy to assume that the feet would lie at the opposite end.
He also assumed that they would probably be a lot lower down and so
we left him to start removing some of the soil which lay over the
bones. Almost immediately we had a call from Andy to say that we
had better come straight back and take a look at what he had found
just below the surface of the soil. Another skull...

As Andy trowelled away the soil (getting rid of it being the only
problem with the excavation taking place in the warehouse), what
emerged seemed at first to be just a jumbled mass of bones. Gradually
it became possible to see some order, although at first we could not
believe what we were seeing. There was one entire skeleton and the

individual bones of another, but it was what had happened to the disturbed skeleton that we found difficult to understand. Eventually, after much deliberation, we decided that we could piece together the story of what had happened in the sarcophagus since it was first placed in the ground over 1600 years ago.

It appeared that the first skull we had seen did not belong to the first occupant. The body of this person had lain in the sarcophagus for long enough to be reduced to dry bones before it was rudely disturbed when the lid was taken off. Most of this person's bones were taken out and presumably stacked by the side of the grave, leaving only those from the knees downwards still in place. A second body was then placed in, its feet obviously at a slightly higher level because of the original occupant's legs, and the remaining bones of the first burial were neatly and carefully arranged over and around the second body. This was the strangest part of what we were observing. The skull and pelvis of the first occupant were placed on the legs of the new body, the femurs (thigh bones) were laid across its waist and neck and other bones were placed in neat piles. What could this mean? Was it simply respect for the disturbed person or were there elements of some incomprehensible ritual involved?

Cleaning the bones in order to take the photographs and make the drawings that form such an important part of the record of a burial was not easy for Andy. With a complete skeleton there is at least the knowledge of anatomy to tell which bones to expect next, which joins on to the one that you have just found. With the jumble of the disturbed skeleton, there was no telling which bone would pop up where; and separating some components of the two skeletons, particularly the tiny toe bones of the four feet which all lay in a mass at the end of the sarcophagus, was a real problem. Nothing for the afterlife appeared to have been buried with either of the bodies although, while he was trying to work out which toes belonged to which burial, Andy did notice and carefully collect dozens of tiny rusty iron nails. When both burials were finally removed and the sarcophagus, still on its cradle and held together with strapping, was finally swept out, there was one last surprise. Running down its full length was a meandering crack, invisible until now, and we realized how close we had been to the catastrophic collapse that we had all feared.

It is not uncommon in the Roman period to find two burials in the same grave, but never before, to our knowledge, had two burials been found in the same sarcophagus and the odd arrangement of bones just added to the mystery. Who were these people? Why were they buried together? All we had to go on were the bones and a handful of iron nails.

The bones were sent over to the Bristol Royal Infirmary on the other side of town. It seemed an odd place to send people who had been dead for over 1500 years but all was explained when we met Gerry Barbour in the Rheumatology Department. Despite working in a modern hospital department Gerry studies ancient skeletons in her research into the causes and origins of disease. By looking at when a particular disease has occurred in the past and matching the

The confusion of bones which lay in the sarcophagus. What stories would the skeletons of the man and the elderly woman reveal?

patterns to the changing circumstances of the time, we may be in a position to predict when that disease will strike again. Changes in environment, in people's lives or in their economic circumstances can all have an effect on whether a disease will spread. It was quite shocking to hear from Gerry that a disease like tuberculosis, which seems as if it should be something of the past, is now a scourge worldwide, also

reappearing in 'developed' countries – principally but not exclusively among the poor and homeless.

Returning to the ancients, Gerry had managed to reassemble the scattered components of the first burial to have occupied the sarcophagus. She pronounced they belonged to a woman, slightly smaller than the average height for a woman of this time at 4ft 11in (1.48 metres) and aged about fifty when she died. The main evidence for her age came from her teeth. Quite a few had fallen out before she died, some time before to judge from the bone which had regrown over the empty tooth sockets. But there was some additional evidence. Her skull had been badly broken, perhaps due to the treatment when most of her bones were removed from the sarcophagus, so we were not going to be able to reconstruct her face. What Gerry could now do, with the skull in pieces, was to look inside it, searching for tiny pits in the bone which she has discovered are a clue to age. The pits are caused by blood vessels in the skull growing upwards; as a person ages, one appears about every five years or so. Once pointed out, they can be spotted quite easily and, as they are something that appears with age, may offer a better way of estimating age than relying on teeth wearing down and falling out. The main problem appears to be that you need to be able to look inside the skull to find the pits.

Comparing the woman's bones with those of her companion in the sarcophagus, there was a marked difference in size, not surprising as they were of a well-built man about 5ft 9in (1.75 metres) tall. This made him a little taller than the average for the Roman period but, apart from this, an age of about forty-five and some slight arthritis, there was nothing more that this first examination of his bones could tell us. There were no apparent signs of ill-health and, as with many burials, it was impossible to tell what had caused the deaths of either of these two individuals. There were, though, some other questions that probing their bones more deeply might be able to answer. They had died during the Roman occupation of Britain – the Roman or, more correctly, the 'Romano-British' period. They could be assumed to have been wealthy as they (or at least she) could afford burial in a new and splendid stone sarcophagus. But were they Romans, or just rich Brits who could afford a Roman lifestyle? It seemed as if the answer to this question might lie in their teeth.

Archaeologists have long been aware of the amount of lead that 'Romans' could have absorbed during their lives. Their introduction of plumbing (from the Latin 'plumbum' meaning lead), their use of drinking vessels made of pewter (a mixture of lead and tin) and even their use of lead as an additive to sweeten wine all contributed. Once absorbed, traces of this lead can become locked up in a person's bones and can theoretically be measured long after their death. Until recently, though, there have been concerns that modern lead pollution, like that produced by leaded petrol, which migrates from the atmosphere into rain and from there into ground water, might affect these ancient levels. As a result, although some studies have been undertaken of lead levels in ancient bones, there has always been an air of uncertainty over the results.

Paul Budd and Janet Montgomery from Bradford University have been looking into this problem and believe that they have discovered a way to overcome the effects of modern contamination. They have found that lead absorbed during childhood becomes locked into the teeth, more specifically deep into the enamel of the teeth where it is shielded from any lead dissolved in the water which percolates through the ground. Until recently the problem has been how to take samples for analysis from the precise layer of enamel where the information lies. The overlying layers could be chipped away manually but there was always the problem of how to isolate this one layer and of introducing contamination in the process.

Now lasers have introduced a new precision. The tooth to be sampled, which needs to have its enamel intact, is cut lengthwise into thin slices, one of which is placed in a chamber where a precisely aimed laser vaporizes a narrow track from one side to the other. As the laser burns its way across, from the outside through the inner pulp cavity and out the other side, the vapour that is given off is sucked away in a stream of argon gas and is passed through a sensitive mass spectrometer. Here the tooth vapour is continuously analysed to show both the amount of lead and its isotopic value. What this provides is a cross-section through the tooth showing levels of lead at each layer and, from the differing isotopes, a clear indication of the source of that lead. Paul and his team believe that these traces of lead were ingested by the person as part of their childhood diet and that the source of the lead, revealed by its isotopic composition, gives a clue to where that person spent their childhood.

It was fascinating to speculate where the couple in the sarcophagus might have come from. Were they born, not in this outpost of the Roman Empire, but somewhere warm and exotic? Were the amphorae full of wine and olive oil to remind them of their childhood home? When the answers came back it turned out that the lead in their bones was from the nearby Mendips; it seemed as if they had both grown up in the Bristol area. The man, though, had a staggering level of lead in his body, over ten times the average modern level. Could this have contributed to his death, and how did he get such a startling amount of lead in his body?

Much to our surprise the answer lay in some of the most uninteresting-looking finds from the excavation, strangely shaped lumps of what looked like rock. They turned out to be slag, the waste products of metalworking, and fortunately Gerry McDonnel of Bradford University found them quite fascinating. On many Roman sites there is evidence for working iron, maybe the equivalent of the village blacksmith of later times, and sometimes bronze and other copper alloys. What Gerry found in the misshapen lumps of slag from Mangotsfield was evidence for a much wider variety of metalworking, in iron, copper and lead. Such variety in one place is unusual in itself and at first it was far from obvious what sort of lead working had been carried out. After the lumps of lead slag were sawn through and examined under a microscope, the crystal patterns pointed to some sort of smelting, but for what reason? It was only when Gerry looked at a sample under a scanning electron microscope at a magnification of 5000 times that he realized what the Roman smiths had been doing. The high-power microscope helped him to spot little specks of impurities in the lead which the machine identified as copper and silver. What Gerry had was 'lithage', a peculiar sort of slag which occurs only when a smith is trying to separate precious metal from something less valuable such as copper. Gerry explained how the process works. If metalworkers had some damaged brooches, made of copper or bronze but with some silver decoration, and they wanted to recover the silver, then they had a problem. If they simply melted the object then the silver would be dissolved in the other metal and would be lost, so they used a process whereby the brooches were put into molten lead, the whole lot was melted together and air was blown over the resulting mixture. The lead oxidizes out and takes away the copper, leaving a little blob of pure silver. If this was what was going on at Mangotsfield then could the source of our man's wealth be jewellery manufacture or repair? It was a distinct possibility.

This left only those tiny rusty nails that we had found around the man's feet at the end of the sarcophagus. When we looked at them more closely there were fragments of what looked like leather still attached to them, preserved by the rusting of the iron. Mark Corney knew just what they were: all that remained of some Roman footwear, not boots as you might obviously think when confronted with hobnails, but more like thick-soled sandals. Like all the metal objects from the site the tiny nails had been X-rayed; this had shown that they were tin-plated, perhaps a sensible precaution to prevent them rusting. Armed with a handful of new hobnails we went off to see Mark Beaby, a craftsman in leather who, from his workshop in the Royal Armoury at Leeds, spends a lot of his working life making shoes, but not the sort for everyday wear. Based on evidence from surviving ancient shoes, preserved in the waterlogged soils of wells and

Replica Roman 'hobnailed' sandals, as worn by the man in the sarcophagus.

river banks, Mark made us a pair of Roman sandals, size 9. As Mark joined the one-piece upper to the layers of leather that made up the sole, the purpose of the hobnails became clear. Not only would they give a good grip (although they must have played havoc with a mosaic floor) but they also served to hold together the component layers of the sandal. The secret lay in the last, the lump of shoe-shaped iron against which the points of the hobnails were hammered and which turned them over, bent back on themselves. Those little bent-over points meant that the layers of leather would not come apart and also made sure that the ends of the nails would not stick into the soles of your feet. As Mark tapped more and more hobnails into the soles it became clear that he was creating a pattern. Not just any old pattern, though – this one was based on a complete Roman shoe found in London which is now in the British Museum. When the sandals were finished we noticed one obvious difference between them and modern shoes. Although they were a pair, there was no left or right: they were both made exactly the same shape. Mark explained that this was how they were originally made; eventually, with wear, they would become moulded to the shape of your individual foot.

From a handful of nails and some fragments of preserved leather we now had a clear idea of what our man would have worn on his feet, but why bury him with his sandals on? Mark Corney explained that while sometimes shoes were worn by the dead person, they are also found carefully placed down by the feet, perhaps as a symbol of the long journey to the afterworld. If the sandals really were like the heavy-duty ones Mark Beaby had made for us then this journey must have been long and hard.

A picture was starting to emerge of the man and his life, but what had he looked like? Fortunately the sarcophagus had protected his bones not only from physical damage but also from the effects of the acidic soils on the site. Had he not been buried in a limestone box then his bones, and those of his companion, would have dissolved completely. His skull was almost perfect and Robin Richards was able

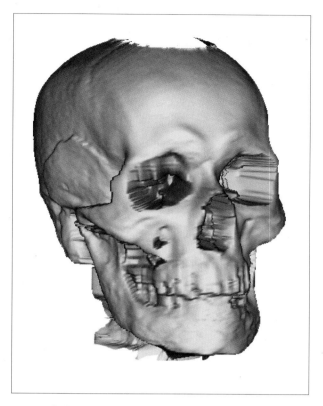

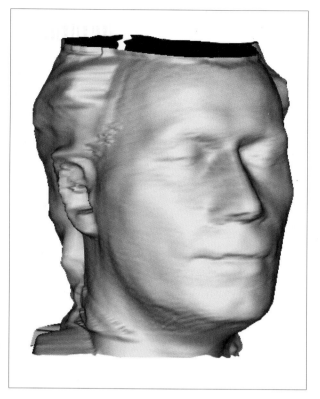

Despite the hostile soils on the site at Mangotfield, the man's skull, shielded by the limestone sarcophagus, had survived in excellent condition and could be scanned without requiring repair.

The addition of an average 45-year-old face to the contours of the man's skull produced a face that, although well proportioned, lacked any 'classical' features.

to use it as the basis for one of his computer-generated images. It was then up to Jane Brayne to create from this a human face, with all the uncertainties that this involved.

There will always be a degree of guesswork when producing a coloured representation of a face from the past. What colour were our man's eyes and hair, how was his hair cut, was he clean-shaven or bearded? At least by the Roman period there are a few more clues, mainly from portraits and descriptions of dress and hairstyle. Jane decided that our man would be clean-shaven, with dark short-cropped hair, turning a distinguished grey in deference to his age. He wears not a toga, out of fashion by this time, but a dalmatic, a type of

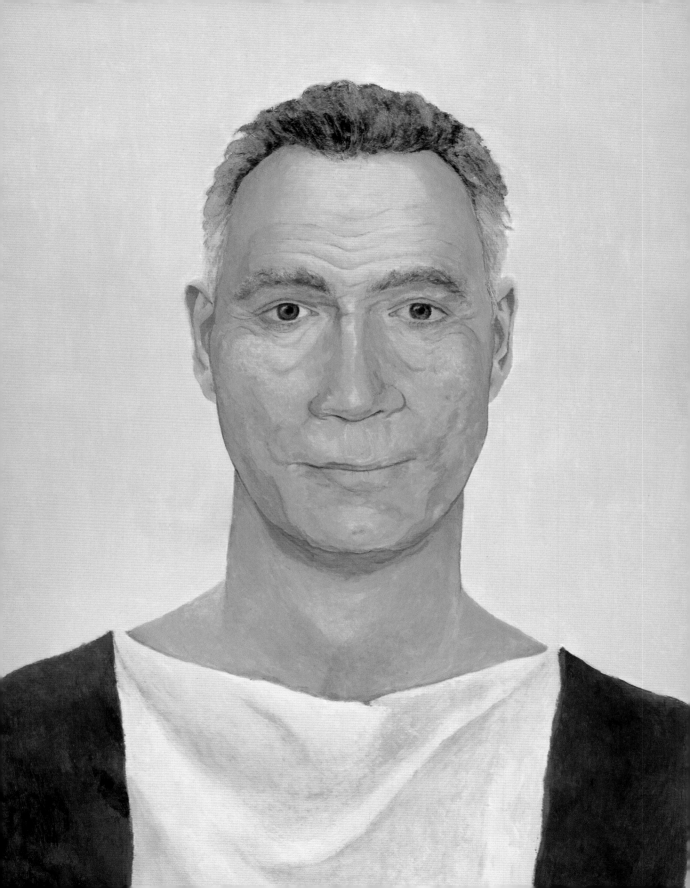

simple tunic that was worn all over the Roman Empire by people of some status. It was fascinating to be able to establish, from historical references, the type of garment that someone would have worn. It helped to create the feeling of a person, and I felt that by now we had come to know quite a lot about the man from the sarcophagus. We know that he was not a Roman but a local man, brought up probably quite close to where he was eventually buried. He was a man of some wealth who had adopted a Roman lifestyle and had a lavishly Roman burial. The dreadful signs of lead pollution in his bones suggest that he may have been a metalworker, perhaps involved in repairing jewellery or in making fine objects like the lovely folding knife discovered on site. How he died we do not know, but one thing is certain: when he died he chose to be buried alongside someone, the woman with whom he shared the sarcophagus. Archaeology and science can bring so much of the past to life, but there is nothing that can define for us the bond that must have existed between them, the bond which finally drew them together in death.

Roman in lifestyle, a Briton by birth, the man from the sarcophagus who chose to share his last resting place with a mystery woman.

AT THE SIGN OF THE EAGLE

ON THE OUTSKIRTS of Winchester, in the disused car park of the now derelict Eagle Hotel, Paul McCulloch and Steve Teague stood and watched as a JCB digger dug a deep trench through tarmac, brick rubble and dark soil. Finally, more than a metre below where they stood, the bucket hit hard white chalk and there, just as they had predicted, were the outlines of neat rows of long chalk-filled pits. What were they? The graves of Winchester's Roman inhabitants.

The car park, conveniently located a mere two minutes' walk from the train station, was earmarked as the site of a small development of luxury flats, but it was clear that the developers had some archaeology to pay for before they could get on with their building. They were in a bit of hurry, though, and within two weeks Paul and Steve were back on site, with *Meet the Ancestors* in tow, to carry out a full-scale excavation.

Driving to Winchester on our first visit, we suddenly became aware that we were heading along country roads that seemed remarkably straight. Could these be Roman roads, perhaps the same ones that legionary feet had tramped? The site, when we finally arrived, didn't look like an archaeological excavation – more like a demolition site, just a very large digging machine, an ever-expanding hole in the ground and a constant stream of lorries taking away the rubble and soil. As the machines worked Paul explained why he and Steve had been so certain about what they would find on this site. The importance of Winchester since Roman times has been realized for centuries but only since 1972 has there been a permanent archaeological team based in the city. The team has carried out a huge number of excavations, both large and small, and has observed hundreds of pipe trenches and foundation holes. The information from these windows into Winchester's past have enabled them to build up a map of the city, a map that can now help them to predict where development will have an impact on important archaeological remains. Paul knew, before he dug his first trenches, that previous developments to the north had revealed parts of a huge cemetery dating largely to the fourth century AD, the last century of the Roman occupation. Between 1967 and 1971 over 450 burials had been excavated and he expected more from the new site at the Eagle Hotel.

Although it seemed quite a small area to excavate, Paul predicted about twenty-five more graves from the old car park and, as the area of machine-stripped chalk was trowelled clean and the grave outlines became clear, it seemed as if his prediction was correct. The graves all seemed to be aligned in an east–west direction and were certainly arranged in neat rows. There was even a wider gap between two of the rows that looked exactly like a pathway running through the cemetery. Perhaps slightly more worrying was a row of large circular pits that ran up one side of the area to be excavated. Paul thought that they might be rubbish pits of a later date, perhaps late Saxon or medieval, and they had certainly disturbed some of the Roman graves.

There was no time to waste in contemplation, though. The piling rig was arriving in three weeks' time and Paul's team had a tight schedule. It was time to start digging.

The first job was to examine the pits. Paul was right: they were Saxon in date and the odd human bone mixed in with the rubbish that filled them showed that they had sliced though the earlier burials. What had the Saxon pit-diggers thought as they cut through old bones? Were they worried by them? Had they any idea how old they were? With the pits excavated it was clear what a narrow escape some of the Roman skeletons had had. Some had lost no more than their toes and one man lay intact in the narrowest strip of undisturbed ground between two deep pits, in the sides of both of which his bones were clearly visible.

ABOVE: *With the accumulated soils and debris of centuries stripped away, the outlines of graves showed clearly in the white chalk.*

RIGHT: *A narrow escape for this Roman skeleton which lies exposed in the side of a Saxon rubbish pit, dug through the cemetery 600 years after the burials.*

As the timetable for the excavation was very tight, I was soon pressed into service and given a grave to excavate, aligned east–west but smaller than most and with an unusually chalky filling. I found out why when it turned out not to be a grave but a hole for a very large wooden post, one of a cluster which formed the ground plan of a Saxon timber building. This was an unexpected bonus and explained why all those pits had been there – somewhere to get rid of your rubbish in the days before the council did it for you. The main reason for the excavation was to examine the cemetery, though, and this is what we started to do, for a couple of days anyway. The old hotel that stood next to the excavation had always looked rather derelict but, suddenly, large cracks started to appear on its back wall and there was real concern that the whole building could collapse. If it did then there was only one way it could go: into the excavation trench. Despite our protestations, we were all ordered off the site by the safety officer and told to come back when the buildings had been shored up.

At least this interlude gave us time to find out more about Roman Winchester and why the cemetery that we were hoping we would finally get to see excavated was located where it was. Back at the headquarters of the Winchester Archaeological Unit, Steve showed me their computer mapping system, which brings together all the information from their decades of work in the city. The modern city of Winchester lies in a fertile chalk valley, at a natural crossing place on the River Itchen, an ideal location that had not been overlooked by the prehistoric inhabitants of the area. Next to the river crossing lay a large ditched enclosure known as 'Oram's Arbour', perhaps the home of an Iron Age tribe known as the Belgae. Oram's Arbour may indeed have been the 'market place of the Belgae', the place that gave Winchester its Roman name of 'Venta Belgarum'. When the Romans arrived their impact was immediate and permanent. The outline of their town, which can still be seen in the street pattern of today, partly overlapped the old Iron Age enclosure and involved tidying up the course of the river in the bottom of the valley. Rather than the meandering streams that once flowed haphazardly across the wide flood plain, one canalized course now formed the edge of the new Roman town. Nothing could stand in the way of their planning. The first town defences were of earth and, from each of the five gates, roads marched out across the surrounding countryside. Straight and well constructed, four of the roads linked Venta Belgarum with Calleva (Silchester) to the north, Corinium (Cirencester) to the north-west, Sorbiodunum (Old Sarum) to the west and Clausentum (Southampton) to the south. Communications were very important and, once these roads were established, Winchester was truly a part of the Roman Empire.

Winchester High Street, laid out by Roman town planners over 1900 years ago.

Within the town a grid of streets was laid out, dividing the defended space into separate 'insulae', some for important civic buildings such as the forum or the temple, others for houses and shops. It was strange to walk up the High Street in Winchester and know that it was on the line of the main Roman street through the town. On this same line, way below the modern pavement, the boots of Roman legionaries had tramped over 1900 years ago. Stranger still is the fate of Winchester's Roman walls. Only two sections now survive: one, a sad and crumbling fragment, lies close to one of the main gates on the eastern side of the town. The other, found while a house was being renovated, sits protected by a glass panel under a carpet in the sitting-room of a terraced house.

This picture of the Roman town had been built up through years of observation and excavation, work which had also revealed many of its Roman inhabitants. With the exception of the occasional infant found buried within the circuit of the defences, most lay in large cemeteries outside the walls, often alongside the main roads. This pattern fits well with what we know of Roman law that forbade burial within the city, with the exception of infants. The reasons for such a law were both practical and spiritual: there was no desire to pollute in any way what was seen as the world of the living with the remains of the dead. This explained why our cemetery lay where it did and why so many burials had been found just beyond the line of the walls on this side of town.

As the excavation progressed, deeper graves containing well-preserved burials were found towards the centre of the site.

Enjoyable though the exploration of Roman Winchester had been, we were all impatient to resume work on site and it was a great relief when the crumbling hotel was finally declared safe and we were allowed to return. The first part of the site that we had been working on had, in some ways, been a little disheartening. Most of the burials that we had

seen so far had been disturbed by the Saxon pits, or lay half under the edges of the excavation trench. The weather had also been atrocious, rain and sleet making the surface of the chalk as slippery as an ice rink. But our patience was rewarded and the next area to be excavated seemed to contain undisturbed graves.

Like the disturbed graves that we had already seen, they were all aligned east–west, but there the similarity ceased. As, one by one, the skeletons within the graves were exposed, they started to show a remarkable variety of attitude and method of burial. One lay in the base of a deep chalk-cut grave with rough flint nodules forming a 'pillow' around its head. Others lay with their feet so tightly together and their arms so closely by their sides that the body must have been firmly wrapped in a shroud when it was buried. Most skeletons lay on their backs but some were buried in a prone position, face down in the grave. Children were buried alone, or their small graves were cut into adult graves – perhaps those of their parents. Strangest of all was the grave that contained an otherwise complete skeleton which at first appeared to be missing its skull. This turned out not to be missing, just to be down by the knees, somehow not the place where you would expect to find it. This we found out was a 'decapitation' burial, evidence of a practice in which the head is removed from a body after death and buried in the grave, often in the position that we had found. What was the idea behind this? Our Roman expert Mark Corney explained that this strange practice was unlikely to be the result of execution, which might seem the most obvious explanation. Instead it may have been seen as a way of preventing people with certain 'powers', maybe no more than a strong personality, from returning from the dead.

We also wanted to know why there were so many different types of graves within one cemetery. According to Mark, the reason for all the graves lying in the same direction could be due to the fact that Christianity took over as the official religion of the Roman Empire during the fourth century AD. This new religion dictated that the

body was buried in a specific way, aligned east-west, in order that it
would be facing in the right direction on the day of resurrection.
What was apparent at this time, though, is that some people,
although nominally Christians, were hedging their bets when they
died and were carrying on with some distinctly pagan practices.
People were often buried with coins placed in their hand or mouth,
intended to pay Charon the ferryman for carrying them over the River
Styx to Hades.

Right on cue Malcolm Gomersall, one of the digging team, found
the grave of a small child, buried in an east–west direction but with a
coin in the soil which filled it. The coin seemed in remarkable condition the first time we saw it. Unfortunately this also turned out to be
the last as that night the site store was broken into and the coin,
together with other finds and all of the site's photographic and sur-
veying equipment, was stolen. This was a tremendous blow. Equipment can be replaced but a find like the coin has far more value than
whatever it can be sold for: as a clue to the past, each object is price-
less. Fortunately we had filmed the coin as soon as Malcolm found it
and, from the images we had recorded, Paul was able to identify it as
being of the Emperor Valentinian and dating to between AD 364 and
375. All was not lost.

As the excavation progressed further, and at a quicker pace as
time on site was running out, we suddenly came across an area of
much deeper graves, some of which were cut down well over a metre
into the chalk. I was given one of these to excavate and soon found
that there was nowhere to put your feet, particularly once the base of
the grave had been reached. The only way to work was perched over
the skeleton with each foot resting on a narrow ledge of chalk hard up
against the side of the grave. When the last of the chalk was removed
from around the bones, it soon became apparent that this grave contained good evidence for a wooden coffin. At the head and feet of the
skeleton were iron nails, pointing in different directions where they
had originally held together planks of wood. The wood had long since

rotted away, although its grain could still be seen in the large lumps of rusty corrosion that had formed around each nail. Even though the boards had gone, their position could clearly be seen in the differing colours and textures

A 'decapitation' burial – the head removed from the body and placed by the knees.

of the soils that filled the grave. Inside where the coffin had been was dark soil, perhaps resulting from the decomposition of the body. Outside was the white chalk that had filled the space between the coffin and the edge of the grave.

The occupant of this grave appeared to be an old lady, missing many of her teeth and with a hip joint that even I recognized as being terribly diseased. The surfaces of both the socket in the pelvis and the ball on the end of the femur were both shiny from wear and dreadfully pitted. It looked like a severe case of arthritis and must have been agonizing.

As I removed this skeleton, other deep graves, many of which had traces of coffins, were also being finished and the whole excavation seemed near to completion. Paul was concerned that there was one area of the site that needed re-examination. In the same area where Malcolm had found the child buried with the coin were the signs of something large and rectangular dug into the chalk bedrock. It was easy to dismiss it as yet another of the Saxon pits that lay in this part of the site, but it could not be. Whatever it was lay below a grave dating to some time shortly after AD 364 and consequently had to be earlier in date than this.

Malcolm drew the short straw and started to dig out half of the huge pit. At a depth of 1 metre it was still going down and the size of the investigation hole was halved. We all helped to give Malcolm a hand as he steadily disappeared from view but we had all returned to our own little excavations when we heard a shout of 'Lead coffin!' The effect was instantaneous: everyone sprang out of their holes and crowded around to see what Malcolm had found. To the uninitiated it might not have seemed very interesting, just a sheet of rather buckled grey metal appearing from under the chalk rubble at the base of what was now a huge hole, nearly 3 metres deep. But we all knew what he had found: a lead coffin, deeply buried and aligned not east–west like all of the burials that we had seen so far, but north–south. A pagan burial. What would the coffin contain? But more to the point, how would we get it out of its grave and off site?

As more chalk was cleared away from the coffin, it appeared to be in remarkably good condition – only the lid was slightly bowed by the pressure of the overlying chalk. It was also evident that the coffin was a very tight fit in its grave and that there was no room to manoeuvre around it to construct any form of lifting cradle. In came a mechanical digger and, with the coffin protected by stout boards, a huge sloping-sided hole was dug. This gave us the working space that we needed in order to clear away the chalk from the sides of the coffin

Working on one of the deep graves. These contained well-preserved skeletons, many with traces of wooden coffins.

LEFT: *The lead coffin exposed at the base of the large hole that had to be dug before it could be removed.*

BELOW: *All investigation of the coffin had to be carried out wearing overalls, gloves and masks as protection against toxic lead dust.*

and see how sturdy or how fragile it really was. There was one additional problem, though. Even standing at the edge of the hole, we could see that the surface of the lead was covered in grey powder, very fine and very toxic. From this point onwards anyone who worked down the hole had to wear protective overalls, gloves and a mask. As more of the coffin was exposed it became obvious that it was not really a coffin at all: at each of its corners were more iron nails showing that there had originally been a wooden outer coffin. What we had found was in fact the lead liner to this wooden coffin. We could also see the way in which the lead liner had been constructed, the base formed of a single huge sheet of lead with the sides and ends simply folded up and fixed using a mixture of solder and nails. The lid appeared to be another single sheet with its edges turned over in much the same way.

The real debate now centred on the best way of removing the coffin (as we still liked to call it) and if the contents should be removed before it was taken out of the hole. We had already peeped through a small crack in the lid and could see that there were bones inside and very little else in the way of soil. If the coffin were removed complete and lidded, then there could be a risk of disturbing the bones and anything else that might be with them. The alternative was to excavate the contents where the coffin lay, but the base of a large hole in the middle of a building site was hardly the ideal place for such a delicate procedure.

The decision was made when Bob Holmes, the Winchester Museums Service conservator, arrived. He decided that the coffin should be removed as it was, and the sooner the better. Fortunately there was a lot of spare scaffolding on site (left over from the shoring up of the crumbling hotel) and an improvised lifting cradle was soon constructed. With a minimum of drama the cradle and coffin were craned on to the back of a lorry and made the short journey to the Winchester City Council works depot where the museum has a store. Here, among the dustcart repair workshop and the grounds maintenance machinery, the coffin was gently lowered into the museum store yard and we all donned protective suits again for what was to be the most exciting moment since the coffin was first discovered: the removal of the lid. This proved to be easier than we had expected as it was simply laid in place and not attached by solder or nails. As it came off an extraordinary sight was revealed.

Most of us gathered around were used to skeletons gradually appearing as the soil in a grave is removed and each bone is defined and cleaned. Seeing the lid removed from the coffin was like having this whole process accelerated, as suddenly there was an entire skeleton – clean bones lying in the base of the coffin. The skull appeared to be in remarkably good condition, robust and apparently very masculine in character. It lay on its side but had not rolled around inside the coffin as we had feared it might. The rest of the bones were a sorry contrast, crumbling, fragmentary, although all still lying in their correct position, undisturbed by their short road journey.

After a flurry of photographs and a quieter period of drawing the bones were ready to be removed. As we had feared, some disintegrated as they were lifted, showing a crumbly, almost crystalline structure to the interior of the bone. What was both unexpected and inexplicable were odd dark attachments to some bones, particularly to ribs and the bones of the spine. In such an unusual burial environment as the lead coffin, had parts of the body that would normally have disappeared somehow been preserved? Were they traces of muscles or ligaments? We lifted and bagged them carefully before storing the bones in a fridge.

Even when all the bones had been removed the coffin was still capable of springing some surprises. Close by where the feet had lain, perfectly preserved in mineral form, was the imprint of a piece of fabric; even the fold of the cloth could still be seen. Was this perhaps a fragment of the shroud in which the body had been wrapped? More puzzling at first were the small conical objects arranged along the base of the coffin, objects that felt very heavy for their size when lifted. They looked like the stalagmites that form on the floors of caves, and we realized that that was exactly what they were: lead stalagmites formed by water dripping from the lowest points of the bowed lid on to the same spot on the base of the coffin.

As the empty coffin was made ready for its final cleaning there was a certain sense of disappointment that nothing had been found to tell us the date of the burial. But the coffin had one last surprise in store. Lying fused to the lead sheet of its base, just underneath where the right hand

The removal of the lid from the lead coffin revealed a complete skeleton, but only the skull appeard to be well preserved.

of the skeleton had lain, was a coin! The occupant of the coffin had been given the fare for the last journey and it looked like we might have the dating evidence we had hoped for.

With the coffin empty, it was possible to appreciate the size of the sheets of lead that had been cast for its manufacture. Molten lead would have been poured out on to beds of specially prepared sand, giving a roughened texture to one side of a sheet. On the coffin lid was an unusual raised patch, elongated and rounded. Whoever had prepared the sand had left the impression of two of their fingers in its surface and these had become preserved for all time in the sheet of cooled lead. We did wonder whether this was entirely accidental or whether it was the lead caster's personal mark, a sign of a job well done.

Bob seemed as keen as we were to find out the date of the coin from the coffin and so, after it had been carefully prised off, assisted by a little weak acid, he cleaned and X-rayed it so that we could have a proper look. The coin turned out to be of the reign of the Emperor Constantine, who ruled between AD 313 and 337. Fortunately this particular coin could be tied down even closer: it had been minted either in 316 or 317. What we had to be careful to remember was that the burial could not therefore be any earlier than AD 316, but it could be later and simply include an old coin. It did suggest, though, that this burial was perhaps fifty years earlier than the one of the child with the coin that had lain directly above it – fifty years in which there had been a change from paganism to Christianity. Strange then that this coin, from a pagan burial, was of the very emperor who introduced Christianity into Roman Britain.

Bob had also examined and photographed the textile impression from the coffin and could tell us that the threads were of linen or wool, finely woven in a weave known as 'extended tabby'. It seemed most likely that it was a part of the shroud as we had at first thought. By now we were all very keen to find out about the person in the coffin and anxious in case the fragile bones had crumbled even more after their removal from the coffin. The bones were going to be examined by Paul Bright, the Winchester Unit bone specialist who had originally removed them from the coffin, and we asked if we could invite Margaret Cox to join us and give a second opinion on some of the odd things that we had seen. Margaret is a palaeo-pathologist from Bournemouth University, who has had extensive experience of lead coffin burials and of the unusual and sometimes unpleasant conditions of preservation that they may produce.

It turned out that our initial impression of the person in the coffin had been correct: the skeleton was of a robust male. He was not very old, in fact he seemed to have been in the prime of life and there were no obvious signs of disease or of what had caused his death. His teeth were remarkably good for a Roman, largely free of the decay brought about by a diet which, for the wealthy, was often high in sweetened food. Margaret also explained that the grey crystalline material we could see in the inside of some of the more crumbly bones was not lead as we had first thought but something called brushite, simply part of the natural decay process. The survival of remains, including bones, inside lead coffins seems to be very unpredictable and Margaret was not at all surprised by the well-preserved skull and the dreadful condition of the remainder of the skeleton. The strange attachments to some of the bones that we had noticed in the coffin were more of a puzzle but she felt that they were unlikely to be preserved soft tissue. Margaret explained to us some of the more unpleasant aspects of lead coffin burial, such as the foul liquid that is part of the early stages of decomposition. She thought on reflection that these odd dark stains and appendages might have resulted from some sort of 'tide mark' showing the level to which liquid had stood in the coffin before its interior finally dried out.

I was also fascinated to find out if Paul and Margaret could tell me anything about his fellow citizens, particularly the old lady that I had excavated. I had assumed that she was old, purely on the basis that she had lost quite a lot of her teeth before she died, but Margaret and Paul pointed out that this was not necessarily a good indication of old age – she may just have had dental problems. Problems of another sort could also be seen in her jaw, which gave every appearance of having been dislocated at some time in her life. Add to this skull, a 'typical Roman shape' we were informed, an 'ivory osteaoma' (a little hard bump in the bone of her forehead) and, to me at least, it seemed as if we had found a very odd-looking lady.

Having been told that her teeth were not a good indication of her age, I was interested in what the rest of her bones might tell us; but it turned out to be a very contradictory story. Her spine suggested a good age, but her ribs appeared to be those of a younger person. One hip, the one I had noticed in the ground, showed signs of severe septic arthritis, but her other joints were in near perfect condition. The problem of determining the age of a skeleton seemed to become more difficult as the examination progressed and certainly showed that it was very unwise to rely on one part of the body to tell the truth. But then Margaret asked why there was such an obsession with calendar age. Maybe this is more a reflection of our modern concerns and would not have been shared by the people whose bones we were examining. For a woman in Roman times life would more likely to have been measured in significant stages rather than years: the first fragile years when disease struck down so many children; puberty; maturity and the child-bearing years; menopause; and the time when independence ceased. It was at this point that I tried hard to stop being so concerned about age measured in years and instead to accept fitting people from the past into broader age groups: young, mature and older.

I would love to have been able to put a face to what I still could not help calling my old lady, but we were now more concerned about the man from the lead coffin. He was clearly someone of wealth and status, buried in such a deep grave in a coffin that we now knew from the traces on the nails was made of stout oak planks. But not simply an oak coffin: those thick sheets of costly lead set him apart from all of

the previous 450 burials excavated on this side of the Roman town. Not one of them had been in such a coffin.

We took the skull of this wealthy man to Manchester, where Richard Neave's first reaction was relief that we had brought him a complete specimen rather than a box of fragments as with Bleadon Man. Richard's first impressions of the skull were that it was of a 'very male male', its masculinity demonstrated by the pronounced ridges of bone about the eyes and the

Outside the walls of Roman Winchester, mourners, musicians and an orator accompany our wealthy man on the start of his journey to the next world.

strong muscle attachments which denoted a well-muscled neck. The face was very symmetrical, with hints of a wide nose, rather 'blobby' and not at all what we would expect from a 'Roman'; deep-set eyes; thin lips, the bottom one probably prominent. Medical artist Denise Smith had been entrusted with building the face and, with all of these tantalizing hints, we were suddenly impatient to see the end result. We would just have to wait, though.

As Denise made a cast of the skull on which to build the tendons and muscles that give structure and expression to a face, we returned to Winchester to find out more about our man's life. From the style of his burial we assumed that he must be a man of wealth and property, but what sort of property? The excavations that have been carried out within the Roman town have shown that plots for houses were laid out alongside the neat grid of streets and on these stood fine houses. Some were built around a courtyard, while others had an elaborate entrance which gave access to a corridor and to projecting wings.

Whatever the plan of the house, at least some of the floors would have been paved with mosaics, elaborate patterns formed of tiny coloured tiles or 'tesserae', and there would have been the luxury of under-floor heating. It is easy for us to take central heating for granted, but to the inhabitants of Romanized Britain this must have been a near miraculous innovation and, for the few who actually came from warmer climates, an essential. In one room of a rich house a concrete floor would be suspended on pillars of tiles allowing hot air from a hypocaust (the fire for the central heating) to circulate and warm the room. To make it even cosier, hollow square section flue tiles were built into the walls to allow the hot air to rise up and warm the walls as well. This was real luxury.

It was not just the house and its heating system that were introduced at this time. Although most of the produce that the inhabitants of Venta needed on a daily basis would have been provided by the rich agricultural land surrounding the town, other food and goods came from far and wide. Through its network of roads and its administration Venta was linked to the entire Roman Empire and the wealthy could enjoy a fabulous range of luxury items. Huge storage jars or amphorae came from Spain filled with olive oil, fish sauce and wine, hinting at a Mediterranean influence on British eating habits. Meals of local meat, game and fish (with additional flavourings and accompanying drinks) would, in the earlier Roman period, have been eaten off fine red tableware imported from Gaul in southern France. The lack of such tableware in later Roman times perhaps means a change to a more casual and communal style of eating. From Germany, Syria and Egypt came fragile glass vessels while bronze was imported from the homeland in Italy. Life then, at least for the wealthy, could be very comfortable indeed.

All this luxury has a price, though, and as a pagan our man from the lead coffin had not one but a whole series of gods to placate by worship and offering. All aspects of his daily life would have been governed by superstition and religious belief, some private and personal, some more public. The Emperor was no longer considered to be a god but simply a divine appointment, and the triad of official gods, Jupiter, Juno and Minerva, had largely fallen out of favour. These were the gods of the temple which lay in the northeast corner of Roman Winchester, while a range of other deities were worshipped in household shrines. The Romans' attitude to religion was liberal and, with the exception of Druidism – the practices of which were seen as simply illegal – all-embracing. Consequently, some of the gods our man worshipped would have been local, survivors from the Celtic Iron Age – deities like Epona, the protectress of horses who guided the souls of the departed to the underworld and whose statue was found close to the temple. Others were definitely Roman – Mercury and Mars – gods of woodlands or natural places and my favourite, Silenus, known for his unusual combination of wisdom and drunkenness.

A pagan in life, resisting the new religion of Christianity that was rapidly taking hold at the time of his death, our man was buried as a pagan, according to Roman religion and law outside the walls of the

town. Here, beyond the realm of the living, the cemeteries formed the 'necropolis' or city of the dead, his resting place for over 1500 years until the modern city of the living expanded and reclaimed his land.

Our final meeting came in Richard Neave's studio where Denise revealed the face that had grown from science, skill and artistry. For once we were not certain that here was a person portrayed at the age when he died. The lead of the coffin had caused such strange changes to his bones that he could have been much older than the 'prime of life' that we had portrayed him in. At this age we saw a powerful man, the set of his jaw and the shape of his brow combining to create a face which would not look out of place wreathed in laurel on a Roman coin. His nose, as we had half expected, spoiled the overall impression – it was too broad for him to have had a truly classical profile but there was a power to his face which seemed to sit well with the status we assumed him to have enjoyed in life.

Who was he, our man from Venta, who died not knowing that the end of the Roman Empire was in sight? Was he a part of the administration that ran the town? Did he trade far and wide? Did he own lands and farms in the surrounding countryside? He was certainly wealthy, and by the opulence of his burial deep in the chalk he set himself apart from those who surrounded him. They might have been shrouded and some lay in wooden coffins, but only his was lined with costly sheets of the very metal that had brought the Roman Empire to British shores. Strong, confident, encased in oak and lead, and with his fare to the underworld grasped firmly in his hand, this citizen of Roman Winchester embarked on his final journey to meet the gods he had worshipped in life.

The face of our man from Winchester: strong and confident in life, well provided for in death.

THE WOLF DEN

FRIENDS PHIL MURPHY and Andrew Goddard are cave divers. Every spare weekend they drive up into the rolling limestone hills of northwest England and don a strange assortment of gear. First comes a waterproof dry suit, worn with elbow and knee pads. Then on go the wellington boots and, on top of these, flippers. Oxygen cylinders, dials, hoses and masks provide life support and finally the whole lot is topped off with a helmet to which are strapped an assortment of waterproof lamps and torches. The effect is bizarre, but the reality of the places they explore while wearing this gear is even stranger. The hills are honeycombed with caves, the result of underground streams flowing through and enlarging softer seams in the folded and distorted sheets of rock. Many of the caves are water-filled and dangerous and there are miles of them waiting to be explored.

Phil and Andrew have discovered many new cave systems through diligent searching and patient observation, noting tiny clues that would escape even the keenest eye. More water flowing out of a pool in a river than appears to be flowing into it points to an underground river adding to the flow. Where does it lead to? This curiosity led them to explore a narrow rock fissure in the valley of the River Rawthey, a few miles from Sedbergh on the edge of the Lake District. Draped with ferns and choked with fallen branches, the fissure hardly looked exciting from the outside. Most people would have been put off by the pile of fairly recent animal bones which lay just in the dark and would certainly get no further than the narrow pool of water which lay on the cave floor only about 6 or 7 metres from the entrance. To Phil and Andrew this

Phil Murphy, fully equipped for cave diving.

was the way in to the unknown and they set off down the water-filled passage, in places having to stop to dig through underwater rock falls.

After 120 metres of tortuous progress they emerged into an air-filled underground chamber. Heading into the cave, they took little notice of this chamber but on their way back, having been halted after another couple of hundred metres by a rock fall that even they could not dig through, they noticed that a steep boulder-strewn slope headed back up, towards the surface of the hillside. Abandoning oxygen cylinders and flippers, they scrambled up the tunnel slope and almost immediately noticed bones lying among the boulders. This was nothing unusual — many caves they had found contained the remains of the odd sheep or cow that had fallen down a pothole, and indeed there were bones close to the entrance of the cave that they were in. But then Phil noticed something that wasn't part of an animal. The most easily recognizable part of a human skeleton is the skull, and this was what lay within the tumbled boulders. Once they were over the initial shock, Phil carefully placed the skull in a niche at the side of the tunnel where it would be protected from dislodged boulders which could come crashing down. They then continued to climb, finally emerging at the head of the boulder slope into a small cave, with other passages leading off in two directions. Despite having already found the skull, neither Phil or Andrew was prepared for what they would see as their torches played around the floor of the cave. Bones, it seemed, were everywhere, some obviously human, some

animal, some scattered around and others arranged in what to their first glances appeared to be neat stacks. Where they had emerged from the slope it seemed as if the cave floor must have given way, sending debris and bones down towards the underground stream that had provided them with the way in. It seemed impossible that the cave could spring any more surprises but, scrambling through a narrow passage beyond where the bones lay, they came to another chamber, its roof hung with stalactites, its floor littered with more bones. This was different, though; here were no neat piles of human

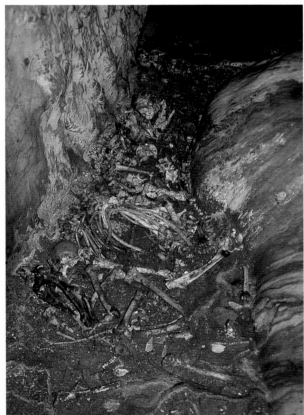

LEFT: *Cut deep into the limestone, the valley of the River Rawthey is honeycombed with caves.*

ABOVE: *A wolf's dinner? The complete skeleton of a roe deer lay against the cave wall in the Wolf Den.*

bones but scattered animal remains, tucked away under low areas of the cave roof and including the entire skeleton of a deer. Phil and Andrew realized that they were in an ancient wolf den, surrounded by the remains of the wolves' prey. As they picked their way among the bones, taking great care not to disturb what they knew was a rare and fragile discovery, Phil and Andrew made their final and perhaps most astonishing find. In the soft mud of the cave floor were footprints, not the prints of their wellington boots but of bare human feet, which seemed to be heading towards the hillside, perhaps to the cave's original entrance. Managing to retrace their footsteps in order not to disturb any more of the cave floor, Phil and Andrew retreated, taking with them only photographs and a growing sense of excitement.

In all their years as cave divers Phil and Andrew had made some remarkable discoveries, but never anything like the Wolf Den. They realized that the remains were not those of a recently deceased caver and that they had made a significant archaeological find. Their first priority was to find an archaeologist who was interested not only in caves but also in burials. In Andrew Chamberlain from Sheffield University they found the ideal combination. As well as being a human-bone specialist, Andrew is one of Britain's leading experts on cave archaeology and had just spent some time studying reports of cave burials discovered during the last two centuries. There were patterns in these old reports and Andrew was sure that the new burials must be prehistoric in date. The fact that there were no complete skeletons and that the bones appeared to have been arranged suggested to him that the burials were similar to those found in long barrows. These are burial mounds which date to the Neolithic period, some time between 4000 and 2000 BC. If the burials in the cave were really this old then he was interested in investigating the cave. There was only one way to find out. Phil and Andrew Goddard made a second trip back to the bone cave with instructions to bring back a specific bone that Andrew Chamberlain had identified from their photographs as being human. This was sent to a radiocarbon dating laboratory at the

University of Arizona (quicker apparently than laboratories in the UK) and a date around 1500 BC was obtained. This put the human burials in the middle of the Bronze Age, not quite as old as Andrew had expected but in some ways more unusual. He decided to investigate the cave with the divers' help and asked the *Meet the Ancestors* team if we would like to come along.

The investigation was planned for the university summer vacation, though the main problem was not recruiting a labour force from the students but gaining access to the cave. Andrew needed to find a way in for himself and his team which did not involve getting kitted out in caving gear and diving through dangerous water-filled passages. He assumed – as our prehistoric ancestors could not pothole, or were at least incapable of a 120-metre dive through a flooded passage – that somewhere there had to be a surface entrance. The question was how to find it. It seemed as if a further dive by Phil and Andrew was called for, this time carrying a radiolocation beacon. From the surface they could be directed by radio to specific points in the cave from where the beacon would send up a vertical signal through the solid limestone. On the surface electrical engineer Bob Makin carried a strange kite-shaped aerial, the location device which would lead us to the divers' position.

The first place to be tried was the end of the Wolf Den, where the original entrance seemed to be blocked by fallen boulders. This led to a featureless area of the hillside going down to the river with no sign of an entrance, blocked or otherwise. On the radio Bob asked the divers to move back into the bone cave, to the point at the top of the boulder slope. Andrew Chamberlain had already become suspicious about the 'shakeholes' on the hillside close to where we were searching. These are large circular depressions in the rock caused by water running down through cracks in the limestone, and often lie above caves. It seemed as if one of them might offer a way into the cave; the question was, which one?

Bob's location device provided the answer, homing in on a huge shakehole a little way up the slope from our first location point. If confirmation was needed that this was the right one, it was provided when we realized that we no longer needed the radio to communicate with Phil and Andrew in the cave below. To our surprise we found that if we listened very carefully with our ears to the rock in the bottom of the shakehole, we could hear Phil and Andrew talking down in the cave. A request for a shout brought the howling of wolves from below, just to let us know where they were. If we could hear them talking then there couldn't be much blocking the base of the shakehole, something that the divers were able to confirm. As far as they could see from their position below ground, the cave sides converged as they rose until the roof was formed where large boulders spanned a narrow rock fissure. Remove the boulders and we were in.

A few weeks later we went back with Andrew Chamberlain and his student digging team to start the excavation through the base of the shakehole. Andrew had allowed one week for the investigation, which seemed very optimistic considering we had no precise idea of how much soil and rock would need to be moved. Scaffolding, planking, a huge old chain hoist, a generator, shovels, picks, a sledgehammer, all had to be carted up to the site. At least, having the Land Rover, we were able to help with the transport, although there was

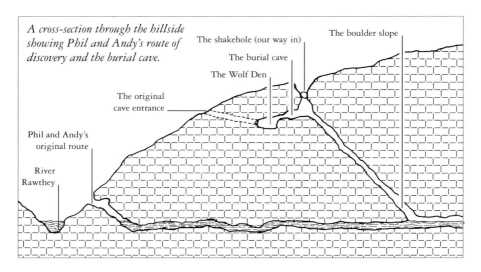

A cross-section through the hillside showing Phil and Andy's route of discovery and the burial cave.

The shakehole (our way in)

The boulder slope

The burial cave

The Wolf Den

The original cave entrance

Phil and Andy's original route

River Rawthey

one boggy patch which even on a first run, on a dry day, looked as if it could be a future problem.

The excavation through the shakehole had to be carried out with great caution as one careless move could send rocks and archaeologists tumbling down on to the fragile bones below. As first the soil and then small rocks were removed planks were placed on the solid rock edges of the shakehole to bridge the potentially unstable area, and the digging team were strapped into caving harnesses roped to stout metal pins. Andrew was taking no chances.

What I found most unusual, after years of excavation experience, was digging down in the knowledge that what lay beneath me was not solid bedrock but just the odd metre of broken rock and then a very large space. Just how large was confirmed when we

The excavation through the base of the shakehole proceeded with caution and concern for the safety of the digging team.

reached the blocking boulders and a small gap appeared. A tape lowered down through the hole showed that the cave floor was nearly 9 metres below and that we were standing on less than half a metre of clay and rock. It was now possible to shine a light down through the crack and see the cave floor below, but there was still a lot to do before any of us would be able to enter the cave. Removing the chosen boulder was like extracting a cork from a bottle but finally, with the ancient chain hoist and a little assistance from the Land Rover, the plugging boulder was removed and we were in.

Although we were all keen to have our first look at the cave, Andrew insisted that he and some of his team went in first to make sure that it was safe and to construct a 'landing platform'. The access hole lay directly above the edge of the boulder slope, the most dangerous part of the cave, and something was needed not only to stand on but also to prevent damage to the bones on the cave floor. This seemed to take an age, more to do with our impatience than with Andrew's abilities. At last we were allowed in, trussed up in harnesses, caving helmets jammed on our heads, down the wildly swinging wire ladder. The first impression was of an extraordinary place, cold, damp, constricted, with beautiful rock formations of flowing stone and hanging stalactites and, everywhere on the floor, bones. In all my years as an archaeologist I had never seen anything quite like this and, for once, I was genuinely quite speechless.

A dilemma that all archaeologists face is whether to excavate a site that is not under any immediate threat of destruction. Until the cave divers stumbled upon the cave it had remained intact for 3500 years and could have remained in the same state for the foreseeable future. Andrew was keen that the cave should give up some of its secrets, but to excavate it and remove its contents, despite the gain in knowledge, would be to destroy what appeared to be a unique site. Andrew decided that his investigation would be as delicate as possible. The contents of the cave would not be removed for study, but would be mapped and recorded in great detail, taking care to cause the minimum of disturbance This meant that each bone had not only to be planned where it lay but also identified, and it was fascinating watching as his team started work. Despite an intensive search no human bones could be found which were articulated – that is, lying as they would have done in the skeleton with one bone joining another. All the bones had been separated and it was also clear that some had been carefully arranged, in ways that hinted at strange rituals. Long bones from both arms and legs were stacked together, a jaw bone lay in isolation and a wolf skull lay inside part of a human pelvis. As the plan was drawn bones could be seen tucked beneath rocks on the cave floor, and as far as was possible these too were drawn and identified. Armed with the plan and his observations, Andrew decided that what lay in the bone cave were parts of three individuals: an adult woman, an adult man and a child who, on the basis of the unfused ends of its long bones, was aged about fifteen. Not all of their bones were present and it seemed likely that the remainder lay somewhere down the boulder slope where they had fallen when the cave floor partly collapsed.

Deeper into the cave someone else was becoming very excited. Ros Coard had arrived from Lampeter University. Some of her students were helping with Andrew's investigation but her real reason for coming was to have a look at the cave's animal bones, in which she specializes. Down in the Wolf Den she had found the evidence that proved Phil and Andrew's naming of the cave correct. There were the bones of both adult and young wolves, together with the remains of their meals, and the evidence seemed to point to 'denning'. The adults were bringing in animals, mainly roe deer, for themselves and also for their cubs. It was the cubs that dragged bones off into the farthest and most inaccessible corners of the cave where they could eat in peace away from the adults. These tucked-away pockets of bones were the most difficult to plan and record as the average human is slightly bigger than a wolf cub. One aspect of the wolves' behaviour was very obvious – there were no signs of gnawing on any of the human bones and so people had not been included in the wolves' prey. What was still uncertain was whether the wolves or the humans had used the cave first, as it is very unlikely that they would have used it at the same time. Excited though she was, Ros had to avoid adding her boot prints to those of Phil and Andrew's wellingtons and the bare human footprints that still lay in the muddy floor.

The footprints were an even greater puzzle. There was no way of directly dating them, but they had to be ancient as some were sealed below layers of 'flowstone', redeposited limestone which had taken hundreds if not thousands of years to form from drips of lime-rich water. If they were prehistoric then they were the only ancient human footprints ever found in a cave in the British Isles. To us, their magic lay in the way in which they brought us closer to a person, possibly the last person who had walked through the cave so many years ago.

The next visitor to what was becoming a very crowded cave was Bill Sellars from Edinburgh University. Bill is a locomotor biologist who specializes in the analysis of gait, the different ways in which animals and humans walk or run. If there was a track or sequence of footprints in the cave floor then he might be able to tell us more about the person who made them. It was possible that we would be able to find out the age and weight of the person, whether they were running or walking, and whether or not they had any physical disability which affected their movement. There were three very clear prints and to us they seemed to form a track leading towards the lower end of the cave where a mass of boulders marked what may have been the original entrance. Bill was not so certain but took the photographs and made the drawings which would enable him to carry out his analysis.

With only a couple of days left until the end of the investigation, we decided to explore the surrounding countryside and try to find where the people buried in the cave might have lived. The hills sur-

LEFT: *Deer bones were tucked away in the darkest recesses of the cave.*

RIGHT: *The bare human footprints in the mud of the cave floor were an astonishing survival.*

rounding the cave show few signs of prehistoric habitation or cultivation but an old friend, Mark Bowden of the grandly titled Royal Commission on the Historical Monuments of England, had recently mapped the whole area and took me to see one likely candidate. The ancient settlement at Cautley Spout lies a couple of miles from the Wolf Den, in a sheltered valley below a spectacular waterfall. Inside an enclosure defined by tumbled stone walls the foundations of small stone-built round huts can be made out, their entrances facing out down the valley. There is a tendency to think that views have only recently become important to us when choosing somewhere to build, but our ancestors were more a part of their landscape than we are today. To them a place where they could view the land and the sun, moon and stars which governed their ceremonies was as important as a place of safety. Perhaps this was where they lived, in a valley which provided water, grazing and a great sense of being enfolded by the protecting hills and their magical waterfall.

The next day it rained. The team in the cave continued with their planning and recording and we spent the day trying to dig the Land Rover out of the bog which had finally claimed it. Eventually we had to admit defeat and were greatly relieved when a local farmer arrived in his tractor and pulled us out.

Back at the cave on the last day before it was resealed, Phil turned up and volunteered to go down the boulder slope to see if he could find the human bones he spotted on his first trip. Although, as far as possible, Andrew wanted to leave the cave just as he found it, he accepted that the bones on the boulder slope were in a very vulnerable position and would probably not survive the next rock fall. It was a hazardous task, and as Phil disappeared backwards on the end of a rope he warned us that there would probably be a lot of rocks falling down with him. Just as he was getting towards the end of the rope we heard a shout from Phil of 'Found it!' and as he finally reappeared he triumphantly informed us that he had recovered the skull from the safe place where he had hidden it all those months ago.

As the bag of bones was hauled up to the surface there was a queue for the ladder – we were all desperate for a look. What Phil unwrapped in the sunshine was an amazing survival: the front part of a human skull, missing its lower jaw but with the fragile facial bones surprisingly intact. None of us could understand how something so fragile could have survived falling that great distance down the rock slope, but Andrew Chamberlain explained that the skull must have been fresher at the time of its fall. A complete dry skull, like the fragment that Phil had recovered, would have smashed into many pieces but flesh and tissue would protect the bone from damage. Andrew's first reaction was that this was the skull of a woman and, assuming that all the burials in the cave were made at the same time, he reasoned that she died in the middle of the Bronze Age.

The only thing that now remained was to plug the cave with boulders and stones and finally to camouflage the base of the shake-hole with earth and turf. Once again the burial cave was sealed as it was when boulders blocked its original entrance so many years ago.

The cave had been a most unusual experience and it was clear that there were going to be unusual aspects to the work that would now be carried out. For a start there were few actual objects to study, only the skull and a few fragments of animal bone which had been collected in order to obtain some additional radiocarbon dates. These, it was hoped, would finally answer the question of who was in the cave first, the humans or the wolves. How much of a picture could emerge from this meagre collection of objects and the notes, drawings and photographs which now formed the record of the investigation?

To reconstruct the woman's face was going to be a challenge, and it was with some trepidation that we took the fragment of skull to Richard Neave. If anyone could rebuild her face then Richard was surely that person, but could he work with so little? Despite some concern about the loss of the lower jaw, which alters the overall proportion of the face, Richard felt – much to our surprise – that there was sufficient to build on with some confidence. When the bone first emerged from the cave it had been damp and very soft but once dry it had become very brittle. Even before Richard made the casts which he needed to work on, the skull needed to be consolidated to prevent its total disintegration. Ready to start, Richard needed to know how old she was when she died. This was not just curiosity on his part – he needed to know in order to calculate tissue depths and eventually to give a sense of age to the face. Here we had another problem, as determining the age of a person from their bones involves a number of observations of different parts of the skeleton and all we had was part of the skull. There

Back in the sunshine, cave diver Phil Murphy proudly showed me the delicate fragment of skull which he had retrieved from the boulder slope.

was one way to find out from the bones that we did have but it would involve sacrificing one of the few teeth that the woman had left.

At the University of Wales School of Medicine, forensic dentist David Whittaker has refined a method of determining age which involves measuring changes in teeth. The principle of his method is quite simple. From the age of about twenty-five, teeth start to die and the healthy, living part of a tooth looks very different from the dead part. Under a microscope the healthy tooth is opaque, but, spreading upwards from the root, the tooth takes on a transparent, glass-like appearance. By measuring how far up the tooth this glassy change has progressed, the age of the individual can be calculated. To carry out the measurement the tooth needs to be sliced but ancient teeth, like those from the cave, can be very brittle and are consequently first embedded in a block of solid resin. Only then can the tooth be mounted on what looks like a tiny bacon slicer

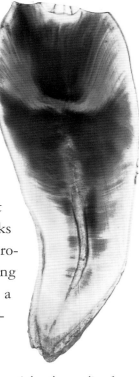

A lengthways slice of one of the woman's teeth. Changes in the tooth structure suggest that she died at the age of about 48.

which produces a sliver one-tenth of a millimetre thick. Using this method David estimated that the woman from the Wolf Den was about forty-eight when she died, give or take about six years.

With David's calculation of the woman's age, Richard could now carry on with rebuilding her face. Watching the way he applied the clay muscles to the plaster cast of the skull, to which he had added the cast of a jaw which hinged on the upper part of the skull and which he felt was an appropriate shape, we realized how important it was to understand anatomy. The final coat, which Richard likened to plastering, needs a different understanding, of the way in which the human face ages. The 'plaster' can be left quite rough if the person is as old as our woman, but needs to be smoothed to a 'peachy bloom' for the face of a younger person. We left Richard preparing for the final stages and went north to see what Bill Sellars could tell us about the footprints.

Bill's laboratory is in an extraordinary building, the School of Anatomy at Edinburgh University. Not every lab we visit has two ancient elephants' skeletons in the entrance lobby. The first thing Bill showed us when we arrived was a computer-generated animation of a human walking. This type of animation can be used to analyse gait when a sequence of footprints is available, and it immediately raised our hopes about the prints in the cave. Unfortunately, when he studied his photographs Bill had found that they did not form a sequence; they had been made by at least two different people. This was quite obvious when we looked at the two clearest prints – they were not only at odd angles to each other but were also of different sizes. Both appeared very small, though, and when Bill measured them and converted the lengths into modern shoe sizes we were astonished to find that they belonged to children of about five and eight years old.

This was fascinating information but there was more that Bill could tell from the prints, particularly the type of action which made them. Walking will create a flat print with an impression of the whole foot from toes to heel, whereas running will leave little if any heel impression. The best prints from the cave showed the individual toes very clearly as well as impressions from the heel, so it appeared as if the children were not running but walking slowly towards what we had assumed was the original but now blocked entrance to the cave. What were they doing in the cave? Had they been caught in the rain while herding animals, or were they just exploring, drawn by the same curiosity that children have today? Had they perhaps been warned by their parents not to go anywhere near the cave, and did children in prehistory take as much notice of their parents as they do today? Perhaps some things never change, or maybe their visit to the

cave had a more serious purpose. They could have been visiting the graves of their ancestors.

Was the face that Richard had now completed one of these ancestors? From such small fragments a person had emerged: a woman with a great strength and serenity that fitted well with her years. The lines and imperfections of age are clearly visible in a face that, as Richard assured me, was not one that he had invented. There would always be uncertainties about the Wolf Den and the woman from the burial cave. Would

Using plaster and clay and his understanding not only of anatomy but of the way a human face ages, Richard Neave breathes life back into ancient skulls.

those she knew in life have recognized the face that Richard had re-
created? Where did she live and why had she and her two companions
been buried deep in a cave? One aspect of her life seemed certain, that
the rugged landscape we had so enjoyed during our stay in Yorkshire
is unchanging in its form and was a landscape that she would have
known as home. To us the hills and valleys are wild and open, places
where we can escape from our crowded cities. To her they were places
which provided food and shelter, grass for animals, water to drink,
wood for hearth and home. Despite the differences in the way in
which we view the land, maybe we can still share with her the sense
that parts of it are magical and, even to us, beyond the explanation of
science.

LEFT: *With an appropriately shaped lower jaw to replace the one lost in the cave, the woman's face takes shape as first muscles and then soft tissue gradually mask the contours of the skull.*

RIGHT: *The face of the woman from the Wolf Den — not a Bronze Age ancestor but one from the Roman period.*

We can speculate about her life, but when she died was she taken on a final journey, from the place where she lived, across hills and rivers to a very special place, perhaps one that she knew in life? There, in the cave, her grieving relatives could have laid her to rest and maybe it was their efforts that sealed the entrance, placing the boulders that assured her rest safe from the wolves that roamed the hills.

POSTSCRIPT

To us this seemed to be the end of the story, of a Bronze Age woman, her life and death. In archaeology, though, the story is never quite complete and in our fascination with gait and faces and the excitement of the cave itself we had almost forgotten about the additional bone samples, including a tiny fragment of our woman's skull, which had been sent for dating to the Radiocarbon Accelerator at Oxford. There had been a few hiccups and the dates were not available by the time the programme was broadcast, but Andrew and I had assumed that the additional human bones would also be Bronze Age. The wolves? They could be almost any date.

Chris Ramsey from Oxford had watched the Wolf Den programme and phoned me as soon as the dates were available. I realized they were not going to be what Andrew and I had predicted when Chris suggested I should sit down while he read them out to me. Our woman had been dated to between AD 80 and 210, and two separate deer bones from the wolves' dinners to the thirteenth and fourteenth centuries AD. Suddenly we had burials dating to the Bronze Age and the Roman period, wolves using the cave as a den in the medieval period, at which point it had still to be open, and footprints of an unknown date.

This is one of the fascinations of archaeology – starting off with a great idea and finding the evidence that appears to confirm it, only to be sent straight back to the beginning to rethink everything when new information becomes available. It now appears that the cave must have been used as a place of burial during two distinct periods, separated by as much as 1500 years. Andrew did not find this at all surprising; it was something he had found records of in a number of other caves. Centuries after this the cave became a wolf den, used by generations of animals that left the remains of their prey littering the floor. The local name of the valley is Ulldale, the 'valley of the wolves', and wolves may have survived late in this area, perhaps as late as the eighteenth century when they are last recorded in Britain. Ironically, we found that the settlement in the valley close to Cautley Spout may be much later in date than we originally thought and may still be the place that we should look to if we want to find where our woman lived.

It was also pointed out to us, with a certain amount of mischievous glee, that if we hadn't been so busy looking for prehistoric remains on the surrounding hills then we might have noticed the line of a Roman road which runs through the Rawthey Valley less than a mile from the cave. Now maybe that was the road we should have followed...

WARRIORS FROM THE EAST

IN SUFFOLK, NEAR the town of Lakenheath, there is a little bit of America – an air base, where huge cars rumble along the roads, the Stars and Stripes flies from the flagpole and where the only currency accepted by the shops is the dollar. RAF Lakenheath is the size of a small town. Twelve thousand people live and work within its perimeter fence and, to make the American families feel more at home there was, of course, a baseball field. But accommodation has always been a problem and in 1997 it was decided, with regret, that the field would have to be built on.

A few years earlier, when a medical centre was being built on the base, some Anglo-Saxon burials had been found and excavated. Although they lay some distance from where the new buildings were planned, there was a remote possibility that the cemetery of which they were part was more extensive than had been thought and that a

few stray burials might be found. Although the base is run by the United States Air Force it still belongs to the British Ministry of Defence and so, when new buildings are planned, archaeologists become involved. In this case the Suffolk Archaeological Unit was called in to dig some

Underneath the baseball field at RAF Lakenheath lay hundreds of Anglo-Saxon graves.

trial trenches and at first the USAF thought that they wouldn't have a problem — until the last test trench, that is. This revealed the faint traces of eight graves cut into the mixture of white chalk and pale sand which characterizes the flat land of this part of Suffolk. This meant that before it was built on, the whole area of the new building would have to be excavated by archaeologists. Fortunately the Suffolk team, led by Jo Caruth, was very cautious and requested what at first seemed more time than they would ever need to carry out their work. It was a good job they did. When the topsoil was stripped from the site the scale of what they had discovered became apparent. Rather than just a few scattered graves there were what appeared to be hundreds cutting into the sand and chalk. They had unearthed a huge cemetery and, when the necessary security clearance had been obtained, they invited the *Meet the Ancestors* team to see what they had found.

In graves that were cut through both chalk and sand the skeleton would survive only in the chalky part.

An excavation on this scale, carried out in advance of a large construction project, needs to be carefully co-ordinated with the builders. The cemetery was divided into zones, to be excavated in a specific order

according to the requirements of the builders. Thanks to the length of time that had been allowed, there was no pressure to finish and move on, just a lot of graves to excavate. Each of the zones was shovelled and trowelled clean, the graves planned and then excavated. As Jo and her team moved steadily across the site, they found the graves of young and old, men and women, rich graves and poor graves, a real community. Some of the men were clearly warriors: two were buried with their swords, which would have been much prized possessions, and others had the remains of spears and the iron fittings from wooden shields. Many of the women were buried with jewellery, brooches and beads that looked as fresh as the day when they were last worn. Great care has to be taken when excavating strings of beads. The thread on which they had been strung would long since have rotted away, but careful cleaning of the soil, combined with photographs and drawings, may enable the beads to be re-strung in their original order. We can then see them as their Anglo-Saxon owners would have, in the same colourful combinations of glass and amber.

As grave after grave was excavated, the skeletons they contained showed an extraordinary variation in their state of preservation. The graves were cut either into the solid chalk or into a deep layer of sand that filled surface hollows in it. Those in the chalk generally contained well-preserved bones but in the more acidic sand they had often disappeared completely. Some unusual sights, with half a skeleton surviving, could be seen where graves straddled the boundary between chalk and sand.

After more than 200 graves had been excavated, and as work moved on towards the dugout – where the batting team had waited their turn during games of baseball – something quite out of the ordinary suddenly turned up. As yet another area was scraped clean, a huge grave appeared, not elongated like all the others but almost square and surrounded by a narrow circular ditch. The ditch showed clearly that this grave had originally been covered by a small round barrow, a low mound that, in a cemetery of unmarked graves, would have set its occupant apart from the rest. Worryingly, though, Jo could see the telltale signs of a modern trench, perhaps dug to take a water pipe, running straight through the middle of the grave. Had this disturbed or perhaps destroyed whatever secrets it contained?

It must be very tempting for any excavation director to pull rank and dig the most interesting-looking grave on the site, but Jo was far too diplomatic (and too busy) to do this. Instead Jonathan Van Jennians was chosen to excavate this new and unusually large grave.

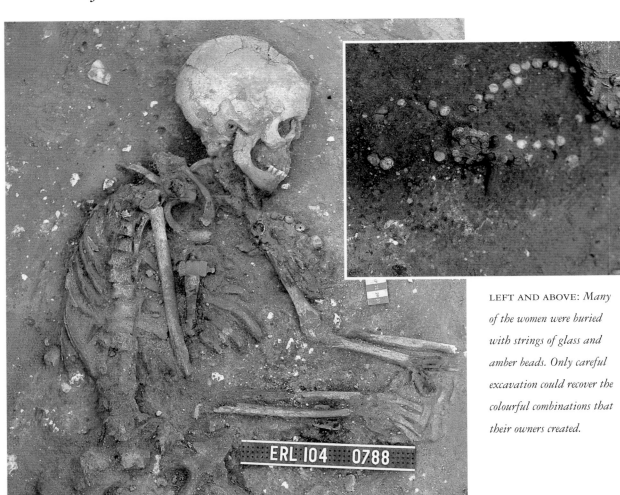

ERL 104   0788

LEFT AND ABOVE: *Many of the women were buried with strings of glass and amber beads. Only careful excavation could recover the colourful combinations that their owners created.*

Experience had taught the diggers that the skeletons in the graves usually lay at least half a metre below the ground surface and Jonathan was consequently very surprised when bone appeared almost as soon as he had started digging. The bone was large and tight up against the edge of the grave. What was it doing there and why wasn't it at a lower level? The reason became clear as more of the bone was exposed. It was a skull, but of a horse not of a human. This in itself was fascinating but it was the small green lumps that appeared lying on the side of the skull and the rusty stain near the teeth that made Jo realize that here they had a unique find. The green lumps were the corroded remains of bronze harness fittings, the rusty stain an iron bit – all, they hoped, in exactly the position that they were when the horse was buried over 1400 years ago. For the first time ever, they had found a horse that had been buried wearing its bridle.

As the harness fittings were drawn and then removed, their position could be compared with the green stains on the bone of the skull caused by the metal corroding. At this point Jo and her team realized that, despite their great care, some of the fittings may have slipped slightly from their position. If there were more fittings on the other side of the skull, how could they reach them and make sure that their position was precisely plotted? How were they to tackle the excavation of the skull? As more bone was exposed it became very obvious how the horse had died. A heavy blow had smashed the front of the skull, just above the eyes. A passing USAF vet confirmed that this was exactly the spot to hit a horse to kill it.

Jo knew by this stage that they were dealing with something very special. A quick glance at the harness fittings before they were whisked away to the conservation laboratory had shown just how elaborate they were. Not only were they finely decorated with delicate patterns, but also glints of gold through the corrosion showed that they had been gilded. These were hints of wealth and prestige but no one could have been prepared for what emerged as the excavation of the grave continued.

As the rest of the horse's skeleton was uncovered, lying on its right side with its neck bent up against the side of the pit, it became very obvious why the grave was quite so large. But the grave had not been prepared solely for the horse. Up against the opposite side of the grave, almost touched by the outstretched horse's legs, was a human skeleton, the bones of someone tall and strong and, from the shape of the skull, very obviously male. As the bones were uncovered corroded lumps of iron appeared, some long, some rounded, some of an indistinct shape; and gradually Jonathan and the onlookers realized what an extraordinary collection of objects this man had been buried with.

Slight stains in the sand showed that he had been buried in a wooden coffin. A spear and shield, neither of which in their original form would have fitted inside, had been placed on its lid. Both these warrior symbols were now represented solely by their surviving metal parts, the head of the spear and the central boss and handle of the shield. When these objects had been removed it became clearer just what had lain inside the coffin. There was an iron knife and some sheep bones, perhaps joints of meat to provide food for the next world. Over his left arm, in confirmation that here we had the grave of a great warrior, lay a huge iron sword, which even when first revealed could be seen to have a bronze-capped handle. Finally, as if to emphasize the link between man and beast, close by the horse's head lay a corroded mass of iron that, with great excitement, was identified as the remains of an iron-bound bucket. Jo's team had already found warrior burials, men with swords, shields and spears, but this grave had all of these and more.

Standing back to look at the grave and its occupants, we thought it astonishing how luck had combined to ensure that they had survived. The pipe trench that cut through the grave, and that had caused so much concern when it had first been noted, had missed the horse skeleton by a matter of a few centimetres. It was also lucky that, presumably by chance, the grave was cut into chalk and not sand, resulting in the bones surviving in almost perfect condition. Strangely, though, the grave with the horse and warrior were set to one side of the area inside the ditch. The other side was empty – perhaps awaiting another occupant who never came?

Many Americans regard Britain as their ancestral home and it was not surprising that the families who live on the base were fascinated by Anglo-Saxon graves emerging from under what had been their baseball park. The excavations had attracted a steady stream of visitors since they started, but the find of this new grave really excited everyone's imagination. Over 2000 people from the base paid a visit to the site and the news of this 'ancient warrior buried among modern-day warriors' was spread worldwide by the USAF's own media network.

Jo's team were elated by their find but, as with most exciting finds, their elation was tinged with concern for the fragile objects. They had not bargained for this incredible collection. How could they be removed from the ground to safekeeping, and what vital information did the flaking rust and stained soil that surrounded them contain? It was at this point that the British Museum offered to help. Angela Care Evans, their specialist in Anglo-Saxon metalwork, had excavated the only other bridle of this period ever found, from the famous ship burial cemetery at Sutton Hoo. That, though, had been dumped in a heap in the bottom of the grave and it had been impossible for her to be certain about the position of the various fittings. Here now, at Lakenheath, was the answer to her prayers, something she had never thought she would see again. Angela explained to me that, although the actual straps are always the same on Saxon bridles, the decorative fittings are always different, maybe simply a matter of individual taste and wealth. Decorated bridles were very special and this one, with its gilt bronze fittings on which she had noted small silver applied decorations, was stunning. What excited Angela most, though, was that the bridle was still on the horse and appeared only to have slipped slightly off centre, presumably when the horse's head rested against the side of the grave.

ERL 104   4116

As well as her experience of bridles Angela brought with her some practical help in the form of part of the British Museum's conservation team. Fleur Shearman and Marilyn Hockey arrived equipped to lift the horse's head, complete with the iron bit and the bronze fittings that they assumed lay buried beneath the skull, in a large block of soil. They intended to take this back to their laboratory where the excavation of the delicate objects could be carried out with microscopic precision. Jobs like this are never quite as straightforward as they seem and, as it turned out, their first task was to lift the remains of the iron bucket. This lay so close to the iron bit in the horse's

LEFT: *When fully excavated, the warrior lay with all his weapons and, perhaps the greatest sign of his power, his sacrificed horse.*

RIGHT: *The true symbol of the warrior in Saxon times — a fine sword.*

mouth that they feared the two had become fused together with corrosion. As the stack of iron rings that had bound together the wooden
bucket was removed, its contents were collected in case there were any
surviving clues about what it had held. Most of us liked to think that
it was the horse's bucket and that, just as the warrior had his joints of
lamb, we would find the horse's last meal of oats.

With the bucket and the rest of the horse's skeleton removed, the
job of stabilizing the head for lifting could start. It was first covered
in aluminium foil and then, with Fleur and Marilyn masked against
the fumes, soft sheets of polyester resin were gently moulded around
the contours of the skull. Once the resin sheets had cured and hardened in the sunlight (or what passed for sunlight on an overcast
autumn day), then the plastering could begin. I have always been very
impressed by the patience of specialist conservators, being prepared to
take days to make sure that an object is as well packed as it possibly
could be. Telling Fleur and Marilyn that 'they must be very patient'
while they were hard at work in a cold damp muddy hole just resulted
in raised eyebrows.

Eventually the head was lifted, now very heavy and unrecognizable under its layers of foil, plastic and plaster. Fleur and Marilyn
decided that as they were there they might as well also lift the sword
that was now looking very delicate. Not only were flakes of rust
falling off it, some of which carried the impressions of wood and other
long-decayed components of the scabbard, but there was a bigger
problem: the sword was actually fused to the arm bone across which it
lay. Angela had also noticed a large bead tucked half underneath it, a
bead to decorate the scabbard, and possibly still attached. Using the
same materials that they had used for the skull, the sword, arm bone
and bead were all packaged and lifted, another delicate parcel for the
laboratory.

The excavation of the grave was now coming to an end and
finally, one by one, Jonathan removed the warrior's bones. Lifting the
skull is always a nerveracking experience and we knew too well that

one that looks perfectly sturdy and solid can crumble like dust in your hands. When the time came to test the warrior's endurance both archaeologists and US Air Force officers watched anxiously. As the skull was lifted we all felt a sense of the warrior's strength and power. For the first time I could imagine what the face of this person was going to look like.

The grave had a profound effect on all of us who had witnessed its excavation, and Jo expressed well what many of us felt. To her, great effort and care had been put into the burial, into making beautiful things; although life then may have been harsh, it cannot have been a brutal existence.

After the huge excitement of the warrior burial there was still the rest of the cemetery to complete and, although some areas were apparently finished, Jo had found that carefully re-cleaning apparently blank areas often revealed additional graves. It was often small graves that turned up in this way and, as a result, two extraordinary features of the cemetery became apparent.

In a number of the small graves lay children, their milk teeth showing that they had died at a tragically early age, perhaps as young as three or four years old. Some, as young as this, had been buried with full-sized weapons, the spears and shields which marked adult warriors. None of these warlike objects would even have fitted into the tiny graves – the spear must have had its wooden shaft broken before burial. Why were these small children buried with such adult weapons? They surely could not be toys. Perhaps each child was destined to grow up to be a warrior but death had intervened, and this was a grieving parent's way of marking what should have been.

As the chalk around the warrior's grave was cleaned again and again more child burials appeared until it was clear that there was a deliberate cluster, centred on what must have been the low mound which marked it. Why was a great warrior surrounded by the graves of children? Were they his?

As the excavation drew to a close the final tally of graves was a

staggering 260 and the huge task of analysing the findings moved
into its first stage. It was very tempting to try to find out more about
some of the individuals we had seen being excavated – the archer with
his quiver of arrows or the woman with her beautiful beads. We were
aware, though, that we really had quite enough to do; for
us to follow the progress of the warrior and his treasures
was going to be a full-time job.

We caught up with the warrior at the offices of the
Suffolk Archaeological Unit where their human-bone

In the British Museum the
horse skull was excavated,
revealing the remains of the
elaborate decorated bridle.

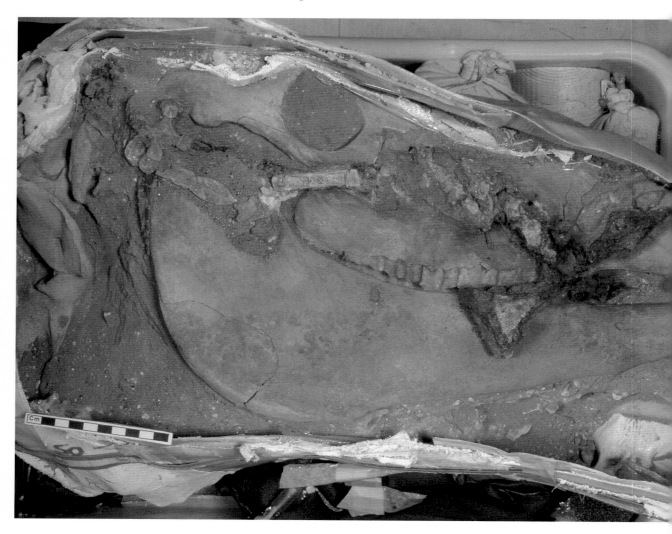

specialist Sue Anderson was going to have her first look at his bones. Our first impressions had been correct: he was tall for his times, about 5ft 10in (1.78 metres), and strongly built. In Saxon times leadership was not hereditary but was probably earned, so being tall and strong would have been a definite advantage. For a robust man of about thirty he seemed to have been in good health apart from some minor back problems. Sue told me that these, showing as traces of slight physical damage to the spine, were quite common in Anglo-Saxon men and could have been caused by lifting heavy weights or possibly by falling off a horse. I was interested to know why a great warrior, buried with so many weapons, showed no signs of battle injury. Perhaps his weapons were just for show, to justify his power in a time when leadership was by no means guaranteed.

Of all the skulls from the site his was in the best condition and showed the classic male characteristics of a square jaw and the large muscle attachments that denote a strong neck. We were curious to see what our warrior had looked like, and so his skull was sent to Robin Richards for the computer scanning which forms the first stage of a facial reconstruction. For the first time, though, we felt that we might have so much information about this man that we could produce not only a portrait of his face, but a full-length one, complete with horse as well. For the second, our illustrator Jane Brayne would need a lot more information about our warrior's clothing and weapons, so we headed off to the British Museum to see how they were getting on.

In the conservation laboratory Fleur and Marilyn had already started to saw open the top of the resin shell which had protected the skull in transit. Fleur now had the distinct advantage of a set of X-rays, taken of the whole block containing the horse's skull, which showed the position of the remaining bronze fittings. Guided by the X-rays, the excavation of the opposite side of the skull, the one which had faced down in the grave, could begin. The advantages of being able to carry out an excavation in the laboratory are obvious and enormous. Away from variable weather conditions, the day-to-day pressures of the site and inadequate light, the excavation can be carried out at a more thoughtful pace. As sand and chalk were removed with dental probes and wooden toothpicks the fittings were revealed and, for the first time, the tiny silver plates that had originally been fixed to them. These, looking like small dark leaves, had mostly become detached from their bronze fittings but lay close enough to them to enable the two components to be reunited. A bonus, one which would make Angela's task of reconstructing the bridle so much easier, was the discovery of traces of leather straps. These could be picked out as dark lines on the pale surface of the bone, connecting fittings and clarifying their original purpose either as links or simply as decoration.

The only thing that remained for Fleur to remove from the skull was now the most difficult and the most delicate. The iron bit lay between the horse's teeth, heavily corroded and, as the X-rays had shown, broken. This was a real challenge, but finally it was eased out and identified by Angela as a jointed bit, much kinder on the horse's mouth than Roman bits but not quite as comfortable as those made on the Continent at this time. The now bare skull could be reunited with the rest of the horse's skeleton and hopefully we would find out what sort of a horse our warrior had ridden.

There is a tendency to associate the term 'warrior' with someone on a huge prancing stallion but this was far from the picture painted by animal-bone expert Terry O'Connor from Bradford University. Terry explained that, although larger than most horses which are found on settlement sites, the one from the burial was still only 14 or 14.5 hands high, basically a fair-sized pony. It was certainly a male, in common with almost all that have been found deliberately buried and, far from being an old, worn-out animal, was aged between five and six – a prime adult and a valuable possession. Since noticing the marks of the heavy blow on the horse's skull, we had all thought that this must have been the cause of death, but Terry thought that this

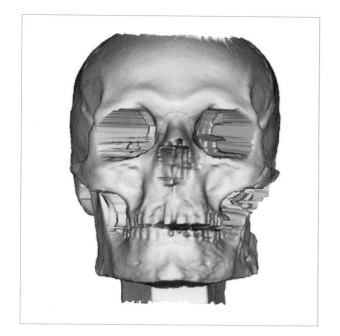 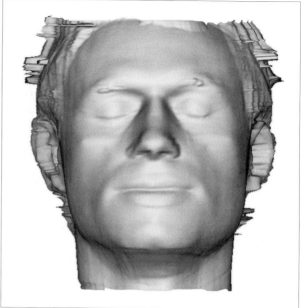

From skull scan to computer-generated face mask – the first stages in the process that would enable us to reconstruct the face of the warrior.

might merely have been a stunning blow and that its throat may subsequently have been cut. Trying to put this somewhat unpleasant image from our minds, we asked Terry what he could tell us of the animal's appearance. He suggested that, if we were looking for a model, we should look for an animal the size of a biggish Dales pony. This should ideally have a rough shaggy coat that would change with the seasons but, as far as colour was concerned, Terry could not help us.

Leaving Fleur to start cleaning her collection of objects, Jane and I set off to track down a suitable pony for the warrior and found Jim, a patient animal that seemed to fit Terry's description. Jim was the same build and height as the horse in the grave but older and, I hoped, quite placid, as I was told that I would have to ride him wearing authentic costume and without a saddle. Unfortunately I am about the same height as the Anglo-Saxon warrior. Although patient, until boredom set in, Jim was also capable of the most extraordinary displays of incontinence and flatulence, timed to coincide perfectly with moments that Jane wished to photograph.

Jane now had both the warrior's computer-generated face and a model for his horse. What she needed now were the details of the horse's bridle and some idea of what the various corroded bits of metal would have looked like when in use. It was time to return to the British Museum. Both Jane and I were aware that the cleaning of the objects from the grave was going to be a very long process and that we could expect only glimpses of their real appearance. The glimpses though were quite breathtaking. There were three main elements to the harness: elongated decorative plates, small rectangular fittings that appeared to lie over points where straps crossed, and long 'danglers' which seemed to be made to swing free. All were delicately carved with interlaced animal figures in a style that Angela could now confirm belonged to the late sixth or early seventh century. We had noticed previously that one of the long plates was quite badly dented and it now seemed that this had lain across the horse's brow, close to where the stunning blow had landed. With the newly cleaned gilt

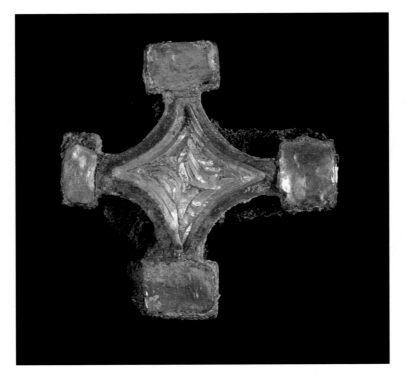

LEFT: *On each side of the bridle, where straps crossed, lay a fitting of gilded bronze, each of its four arms decorated with tiny sheets of silver.*

RIGHT: *A masterpiece of Anglo-Saxon metalwork and the most beautiful of the bridle fittings – a decorative 'dangler' of delicately cast bronze, embellished with gold and silver.*

reunited with the silver of the small applied decorative plates, the combined effect of the two precious metals was beautiful and showed the incredibly high standard of craftsmanship that flourished then.

Even the warrior's weapons were something special. His shield was made of wood and leather, traces of both of which were preserved in the rust of the handle and the boss. In company with most Saxon shields, his would have had a body made of wooden planks over which leather was shrunk to provide extra protection both from blows and from water. The great boss of his shield was made of iron but in the X-rays Fleur had seen precious metal beneath the rust. An exploratory clean showed that the flat head of the boss and the large rivets that held it to the shield were covered with thick plates of silver.

In the laboratory the sword, which had looked so unpromisingly crumbly in the ground, was also starting to give up its secrets. The X-rays which are taken of any iron object as a matter of routine had shown a peculiar pattern in the sword blade. Faint wavy lines could be seen running along its full length, lines which both Fleur and Angela recognized as telltale signs of pattern welding. In Saxon swords of the highest quality the blades are not simply forged from a single bar of iron but from a number of thinner strips of metal, some harder than others. These are heated and plaited together, heated and beaten time and again in a laborious process that results in a blade that is strong yet springy. When new and polished, the marbled effect of this process would have been visible on the surface of the blade, proclaiming that its owner was a man of wealth and a warrior armed with the finest weapon available.

From the flaking surface of the iron blade Jacqui Wilson from English Heritage was able to give us a remarkably detailed picture of the whole sword. If the process of rusting happens quickly enough, as it obviously did in the warrior's grave, then organic material that is next to the iron can be preserved by a process of mineralization. The organic material, such as wood, leather or textile, is not actually preserved, but its imprint and structure are replaced by the products of corrosion. Wood turns to rust but its grain is still visible. What Jacqui found was that the scabbard was made of very thin strips of wood, either poplar or willow, covered with leather and lined with some sort of fleece. This would have served to lubricate the blade with natural oils and so prevent it rusting. The sword handle was made of horn, capped with the small bronze pommel that we had noticed when the sword was first found.

To complete this magnificent weapon its owner had attached a large dark glass bead to the scabbard, a sword bead as Angela explained, there for no other purpose than decoration and yet more proof of status and wealth.

From the first time we had seen the magnificently furnished grave at Lakenheath the picture that had been growing in all our minds had been of someone very special, someone of great strength and presence. Now, after months of work in Suffolk and at the British Museum, the picture could gain substance. Jane's portrait shows the warrior as a man with a broad face, high cheekbones and a strong square jaw. She has shown him neatly bearded in a way suggested by historical sources and wearing, not a helmet, but a leather cap. His fair hair and blue eyes may be taken as implying that he was an invader or settler in Suffolk, an Angle from south Scandinavia rather than a native of this country who had adopted the ways of the settlers and become 'Anglo-Saxon'. In reality, of course, we shall never know.

Reunited with his horse and weapons, our man from Lakenheath seems every inch a warrior. His clothes, based on surviving examples from Germany and fragments of worsted cloth which survived in his grave, are loose-fitting and comfortable. His weapons are effective, his sword the ultimate expression of the swordsmith's craft and his horse, which would not have been ridden into battle, magnificent in its decorative bridle. He is ready for combat, ready to lead. But who was he? Certainly a man of high status, most probably the chief of the people who lay around him in the cemetery.

It was very easy to think of this man simply as a warrior, buried in

a place that 1400 years later would be the home to modern-day warriors, their weapons inconceivable to someone armed with a spear and sword. But somehow to me his image was softened by the children's graves that surrounded his. Was this man with his horse and weapons just a tough guy, or was he maybe the protector of these children as much in death as presumably he was in life?

LEFT: *The Lakenheath warrior and his ornately bridled horse. Armed with sword, spear and shield, he represented the ultimate Saxon fighting machine.*

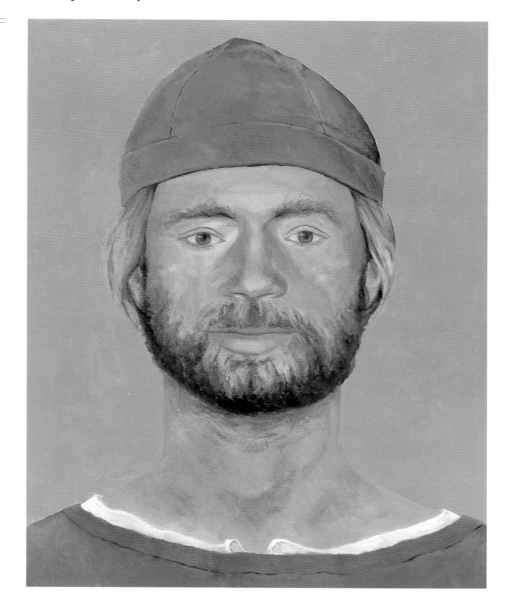

RIGHT: *The Saxon warrior from Lakenheath was the undoubted leader of his band and, perhaps even in death, continued to offer his protection.*

UNDER THE FLOORBOARDS

WHEN BRIAN AND Jill
Bushnell bought a plot of land in Salt Lane in the little Wiltshire village of Winterbourne Gunner near Salisbury, it was the culmination
of a dream, a dream to build their own house in a quiet place. They
knew that they would have to spend months, maybe even years, living
in a mobile home while Brian gradually built the house, but what
they didn't anticipate was the strange story that would start to unfold
as soon as the foundation trenches were started.

When Brian saw the long rusty metal spike poking out of the side
of the foundation trench his first thought was for the tyres on the JCB
digger, so he pulled it out and lent it against the side of the mobile
home that stood by the edge of the lane. It was only when he looked
at it more closely that he realized with a shock that it was a sword,
rusty but unmistakable. Brian immediately phoned the County Council archaeology service and Helena Cave Penny, the Assistant County

Archaeological Officer, came straight out to inspect their trenches. Here began Brian and Jill's acquaintance with archaeology, and with archaeologists.

As soon as Helena saw the sword she recognized it as Saxon in date, and a rare find that confirmed suspicions she had harboured for some while about the early history of Winterbourne Gunner. She had noticed when the Bushnells' planning application had been submitted that ten Anglo-Saxon graves had been found in 1963 at the other end of Salt Lane, less than 50 metres from their plot. It turned out that Jill and Brian should have let Helena know that they were going to dig the trenches so that she could be on site to observe. They had misunderstood and thought that she wanted to see the site after the trenches had been excavated.

Whatever the misunderstanding, there was now a crisis to be dealt with. It was Friday, the trenches were all dug and on Monday the concrete to fill them was arriving. In the sides of the trenches, cut through the white chalk that characterizes this part of Wiltshire, were the unmistakable profiles of graves, filled with slightly softer and brown-stained chalk, and with bones poking out of some.

By the next morning a crew of unpaid volunteers recruited by Helena had assembled on site. A plan was drawn, showing that the graves, twenty-three in total, lay in neat regularly spaced rows and were all aligned in a southwest–northeast direction. As the plan was drawn, trench edges were scraped clean, bones were salvaged from graves that had been cut through and order was retrieved from what had at first seemed chaos. I first saw the site that weekend as AC archaeology, the company that I was a partner in at that time, had lent some of its digging team to help Helena in what was a genuine race against the clock. I remember the discussions about what could be done, not with the graves that had been cut through, but with those that lay, exposed but undisturbed, in the rectangular blocks of chalk between the trenches. These marked the individual rooms of what would eventually become Jill and Brian's bungalow.

How did the Bushnells feel about their startling discovery? Some people would, I am sure, have insisted that every last bone was removed from the site before they would consider living there. Not the Bushnells. Jill was very upset at first, mainly at having unwittingly disturbed so many burials, but both she and Brian quickly accepted that there were burials which would not be excavated and would remain on site buried beneath the floors of their new home.

For an archaeologist a situation like this always produces a dilemma. Archaeologists by their nature have a great curiosity and there was a fascination to know what lay in these undisturbed graves which could clearly be seen as long brown pits in the white chalk. But there was no good reason to excavate them, as they would remain as undisturbed under the concrete of the new floors as they were under the soil of the field, better protected in fact. There was also the sobering thought in the minds of all the archaeologists that what we had excavated and recorded so far would have to be analysed and stored, reports would have to be written and published and that, as yet, there were no funds available for this. We were confident that, having recorded the information that would otherwise be lost for ever, we would be able to raise the money to carry out the necessary analysis. In the circumstances, however, and although it went against the grain, it seemed sensible policy to excavate as little as possible.

This was the policy we followed as work on the bungalow progressed over the next year. Every time Brian wanted to dig a new trench for a drain or to run a cable or pipe into the house, we were there to do the digging. Brian had found a way to turn the archaeology to his advantage – he never had to dig a trench himself again! Hardly surprisingly, more graves appeared and drains and cables carried out all sorts of tortuous manoeuvres to avoid them.

Salt Lane in Winterbourne Gunner, for centuries a quiet backwater that held the village's ancestral secrets.

Back in 1963 the excavator of the original cemetery had found six burials, all with jewellery and weapons, and had thought he had found a rich but small and self-contained cemetery. There were now nearly thirty more burials not a stone's throw away, and the cemetery appeared to be a little larger, if not richer. For what was unusual about the burials that had turned up at 'Hollybushes', the name Jill and Brian had chosen for their bungalow, was that with the exception of the sword and one small iron knife, there were no objects for the afterlife.

In the years after the Bushnells had finally got rid of their mobile home and moved into their new bungalow more excavations were carried out in the building plots that lay on either side of them. More Anglo-Saxon graves turned up, those to the east richly furnished with brooches of many different types, beads of multi-coloured glass and amber and elaborately decorated belts. The total number of graves located grew to over ninety but more unexpected was the evidence that the low ridge had been used for burial since prehistoric times. Traces of plough-flattened round barrows were found, including a rare pond barrow where a circular depression is substituted for a circular mound. It was obvious that these barrows, dating to the earlier Bronze Age some time around 1500 BC, had acted as the focus for the Anglo-Saxon cemetery, drawing the burials with their ancient ancestral magnetism.

With the bungalow and garden finished, Brian turned his thoughts to the garage that had always been a part of their overall plan. He and Jill realized that there was very little chance that something of that size, right in the middle of the cemetery, would not hit some graves. So, after protracted discussions between planners, Helena, the museum and English Heritage I once again found myself watching a JCB digger stripping topsoil and exposing chalk in which I assumed that I would soon be seeing the outline of graves. This was another AC archaeology job and I had come along to help Alan Graham who had arrived with all his digging kit in the sidecar of his ancient BSA motorbike. Jill was out shopping as we trowelled clean the surface of the chalk and, when she returned, it was impossible to resist the temptation to tease her about the number of graves that lay under the proposed garage. Perhaps thirteen was a little hard to believe but it did make the reality, a total of four graves, a little more palatable.

The other half of the digging team – Alan Graham and transport.

As with our first excavation, the idea was to disturb as little as possible, in this case only those graves that lay directly on the lines of the garage's foundations. In the end, we had only to excavate one complete grave and part of a grave that had already been chopped through by an old water pipe.

There are distinct advantages to carrying out an excavation that lies just outside the kitchen door of someone as hospitable as Jill. The weather was fine and Alan and I worked to a constant flow of liquid refreshment, tea for Alan, squash for me. I excavated the incomplete burial, which appeared to be that of an elderly woman. Her bones, like many we had noted in the cemetery, were in a very fragile condition, despite being buried in the chalk that is normally so good for bone preservation. There seemed to be no reason for the state of her bones, although she had obviously been buried in some sort of a coffin. This was evident not from telltale coffin nails but by the attitude of her skull, tilted back and to one side and with the lower jaw dropped down on to her chest. This displacement can only happen if the body is buried in some type of container within which bones can move freely as decomposition takes place.

In contrast, the skeleton that Alan was excavating was male, in much better condition and, with all its bones firmly in place, had clearly not been buried in a coffin. In a burial like this, all that the grave should contain are the bones, whatever was buried with them that could be expected to survive for centuries (pottery or metal, for example), and the soil or rock used to backfill the grave. Here this should have been pure chalk, but Alan became puzzled by patches of fine dark soil that lay beneath the skeleton and particularly around the skull. He had noticed these before in other graves and we could only conclude that what we were seeing were the remains of some form of lining to the grave, perhaps of turf or maybe of grasses or even flowers. Today we associate death and grief with 'floral tributes', but need this be solely a modern association? In the past there may also have been a practical reason. Sweet-smelling flowers or herbs would have disguised the smell of decay that would have been the inevitable accompaniment to the process of grieving. Unfortunately we could not prove this idea as chalk, normally an excellent preservative of bone, also efficiently destroys the grains of pollen that might have provided the clues we needed.

As we added these newly discovered graves, numbers 91 to 94, to the overall plan of the cemetery, they fitted in precisely with the neat rows that we had observed previously. To achieve such symmetry, particularly in the absence of any obvious grave markers, must have required the graves to be visible, perhaps as low mounds of earth, and to be maintained, possibly over several generations.

With our small excavation completed, we handed it over to Brian who carefully laid the concrete floor of the garage over the two graves that we had seen but not disturbed. It was now the time to try to find out more about our Saxon man, a quest which took me to Bournemouth University to see Margaret Cox, with whom we had last worked in Winchester (Chapter 4). I suppose that I had always carried in my mind an image of Saxons as fierce and warlike, but this was far from the picture that Margaret painted.

During the excavation Alan and I had assumed that the skeleton was of a man, an assumption that turned out to be correct. However, as Margaret pointed out, it was a far from typically male skeleton. Instead of large, heavy bones with pronounced marks where big muscles had been attached, the bones were comparatively slender and graceful. There was little evidence of arthritis, the classic symptom of a life of hard manual labour. The skull too was small and lacked the prominent ridges above the eyes that characterize a classically male skull. In

RIGHT: *The newly discovered graves which had to be excavated lay just outside Jill and Brian's back door.*

fact, I was not sure why Alan and I had made our assumption in the first place. Margaret explained that, while over 90 per cent of skeletons have characteristics, mainly in the skull and pelvis, that clearly show them to be male or female, there are a few that fall in between. Slender males and robust females can cause real problems of identification.

Our skeleton was obviously male though, but somehow not what I had expected from an Anglo-Saxon cemetery. There is a tendency to think of all Saxons as being large and warlike but it seemed as if we had found a soft Saxon. In company with many of the burials that we had seen over the course of the year, there were no obvious signs of what had caused the death of a man apparently quite young, and certainly in the prime of his life. But, as Margaret reminded me, there are so many diseases that can cause death so rapidly that the skeleton has no time to develop telltale signs that would survive to be identified. Yet again we were left speculating about the cause of death.

Although our man had no objects by which we could tell when he was buried, it seems likely that the whole cemetery at Winterbourne Gunner dates to the sixth century AD, the Anglo-Saxon period, the beginnings of which are sometimes called the Dark Ages. Britain had long since ceased to be a part of the Christian Roman Empire and waves of pagan migrants – Angles, Saxons and Jutes – either invaders or peaceful settlers, had entered southern Britain. Winterbourne Gunner lies within Wessex, the Kingdom of the West Saxons who originated in North Germany, but how these Saxons lived alongside the resident population is far from certain. Were the residents, essentially the same people who had lived in our islands since early prehistoric times, treated as equals or enslaved? However they lived, it seemed to be very much as they did before the Romans arrived.

Without weapons or signs of wealth, our man from Winterbourne Gunner was buried in a simple grave.

Unfortunately this means that the houses and villages of these pagan Anglo-Saxons are very difficult to find, unlike their burials that proclaim their date by the objects that are often, but not – as we had seen – always, buried with them. No more were buildings made of stone, brick and tile, firmly mortared and provided with strong roofs and heating. These are durable materials that enable the remains of buildings to not only be easily recognized, but also give a clear idea of their original appearance. Instead Saxon houses, even those of the wealthy, were of wood and clay, with roofs of reed or straw. Fine though some of these buildings undoubtedly were, the materials from which they were constructed decay and disappear with time and we are left with little more than a few holes in the ground.

Although Saxon buildings are very illusive, there is one particular form, called a 'grubenhaus', that is more easily recognized. Known by archaeologists as 'grub huts', these are small rectangular buildings with a sunken ('grubbed out') floor, over which walls and a roof are constructed. Some that have been excavated have had the sockets for large wooden posts in the base of the sunken area and, in a few cases, lines of clay loom weights have also been found on the floor. This has led to the suggestion that they were weaving sheds, the posts possibly the uprights for a large loom. Whatever their function, we were fascinated to find that a replica of one of these huts was being built at the Ancient Technology Centre at Cranborne, Dorset. The centre is run by Jake Keen and I have watched with admiration over the years as ancient buildings of diffferent eras have risen in the field behind the local school, many built by the parties of local schoolchildren who come to use the centre.

When we arrived the hut was already half built, the sunken floor dug and the large upright posts in place. Jake explained that so far his reconstruction was on firm foundations, the ground plan and the dimensions of the posts being based on those of an excavated Saxon hut from Suffolk. As far as the rest of the building was concerned, it was a matter of common sense, experience of building ancient structures and an awareness of the materials and tools available to the original builders. Timbers were trimmed and notched using replicas of Saxon axes,

Above the sunken floor area of the 'grub hut', Jake trims the rafters with a replica of a Saxon iron axe.

and rafters of straight ash poles were fixed in place using hand-made iron nails. Making a nail is not as simple a task as it seems, as I found out when it was my turn to make one. It was a good job that progress on the hut did not depend on my nail-making skills. As a departure from thatch Jake was planning to clad the roof with shingles, wooden tiles split from logs of oak or sweet chestnut, their shape based on an example from Anglo-Saxon London. Gradually the building took shape and Jake explained that, far from a damp hole in the ground with a rough shelter above it, he saw the hut as a small but cosy dwelling, its walls of thick turf providing excellent insulation, the sunken area lined with sturdy planks. When we calculated that the roof would take 3000 shingles to cover, we realized that we had a long way to go before Jake's vision could become reality.

If Anglo-Saxon buildings are difficult to find, then the same can be said of the objects that would have been used in them. Many vessels for cooking, eating and storage are probably now made of wood again and also leave no trace. Pots, plentiful, wheel-thrown and well-fired in Roman times, are replaced by a few crude, hand-formed vessels fired on a bonfire and with the impressions of grass and seeds permanently baked into their rough surfaces. All this makes the everyday life of the early Anglo-Saxons a frustrating mystery. How could we understand our man's life when the dead are far more recognizable than the places inhabited by the living?

It was still tempting to speculate where his home might have been, a good excuse for a wander around a lovely little village, trying to imagine it without the modern roads and buildings that now give it form and see the place with Saxon eyes. Winterbourne Gunner lies on one of a number of crossing places on the river not surprisingly called the Winterbourne, which flows due south to meet the Avon at Salisbury. The river would have provided drinking water for people and beasts and maybe a source of power for mills to grind the corn. But the river also acted as a barrier and the good crossing places, where the water was shallow and the river bed firm, would have been well known. It was here that houses may have sprung up, on the dry ground just above the river, and it is in just such a place that Winter-bourne Gunner church lies.

But what has a medieval Christian church to do with pagan Saxons? Although it was built several centuries after our man's death, the ancient church probably marks the focal point of the first Christian village and that in itself is most probably a simple continuation of something much earlier. Find a good place to live and a change in belief is generally no reason to move. The Christian dead lie in the neat churchyard, surrounded by grassy fields, and the humps and bumps in those fields may hold the clues to where our man lived.

In some ways the life of our man from under the garage seemed destined to remain a mystery, but at least we could meet him face to face. Unfortunately, his had been yet another of the skulls that looked so well preserved

Winterbourne Gunner church, the heart of the Christian village, but perhaps also marking the site of the original pagan Saxon settlement.

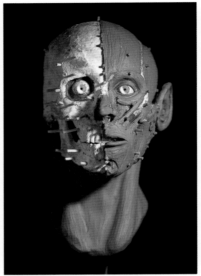

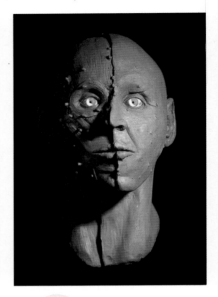

1 *The most striking features of the rebuilt skull were its lopsidedness and the absence of any pronounced male characteristics.*

2 *Pegs and facial muscles start to give an impression of the type of face that will eventually emerge.*

3 *As tissue and skin smooth over the framework of muscles, a recognizable face appears with only hair to be added.*

as it was emerging from the chalk yet had fallen to pieces as it was being cleaned. It seemed strange, but Caroline Wilkinson, one of the medical artists who work with Richard Neave, almost seemed to prefer the skulls on which she was to work to arrive in this sort of condition.

When she had completed her rebuild the most striking feature of the skull was its lop-sidedness. Caroline told me that most skulls and, by extension, most faces are not completely symmetrical, something that she could demonstrate to me with a picture. She showed me what happens if you photograph a face, divide it vertically down the centre of the nose, and create a mirror image of one side. Add this to the other unaltered side and you have a totally symmetrical face that might be assumed to be attractive. In reality it looks most odd and,

'Saxon' or 'native'? The face that finally emerged for the man from Winterbourne Gunner was slightly 'impish' and full of character.

something that can be checked by looking at almost anyone's face, demonstrates that each side of a face is subtly different from the other. The eccentricity of the skull of the man from Winterbourne Gunner was far from subtle though, showing a distinct lean to the right. Not only did the bone of his nose bend in this direction, but his two front teeth were off centre and the socket of his right eye was noticeably higher than the other.

With the original rebuilt skull, a cast of which had formed the foundation for the facial reconstruction, Caroline explained to me some of the subtleties that could be built into the final face. On the skull, just behind where the ears are attached, are bony spines, the mastoid processes, which give clues to the shape of the lower ear. A straight one means that the person had proper dangling ear lobes, one that bends forwards a sign of ears that blend smoothly into the side of the face.

Caroline had warned me that some of the eccentricities of the skull would disappear as the rebuild continued, masked by layers of muscles and tissue. I thought that she must be preparing me for a somewhat ordinary finished face, but this was far from the truth. The face that Caroline unwrapped for my inspection was as slender as I had expected and still bore in its features the lop-sidedness of the underlying skull. More than this though, it was an slightly 'impish' face, full of character, perhaps emphasized by the mouth that Caroline had left slightly open. This gave a more informal and less posed look to the whole face.

This then was the face of our man from Winterbourne Gunner, a slender young man who, when he died, was taken for burial on the low ridge just above the village. Here, where the mounds and hollows of ancestral burials could be made out thousands of years after they were built and last used, he was laid to rest with his fellow villagers in one of the neat rows of graves. But who were the villagers? Were they native Britons or Saxons, or a mixture of both? Was the person with the sword their leader, a Saxon invader whose authority came from the power of weapons? Were those who were buried with rich grave goods also Saxon newcomers? If this is the story that the cemetery is telling us, then does this make our man a native Briton, consigned to his grave alongside others who bore no signs of authority or wealth?

Many of our man's fellow villagers still remain buried on the ridge above the river and, in many ways, they could not have chosen a better final resting place. Jill and Brian find nothing worrying in the graves under their floors and Jill's green fingers have created a beautiful garden out of an overgrown

With Jill and Brian in the garden that they have created, a place of beauty and a peaceful resting place for the ancient inhabitants of Winterbourne Gunner.

sea of rubbish. Whatever lay under the soil behind their house Jill would have worked to make it a place of beauty but she knows of the neat rows of undisturbed graves. That is why the scent of ancient herbs, sweet-smelling plants used since Saxon times, mingles with the headier smell of more familiar flowers. This is why to Jill the garden has to be something special, not just for her and Brian, for their friends and family, but for those that still lie there.

THE LADY OF THE SANDS

THE ATLANTIC COAST of Ireland is stunningly beautiful but the farming here is as hard as anywhere else. Hugh John McGonigle farms fields that run down to the dunes edging Donegal Bay. Sand dunes are no use to a farmer and so, in the spring of 1997, Hugh John decided to extend one of his level fields into the dunes. Sand is no problem to a bulldozer and even the boulders and slabs of stone which suddenly appeared in one corner of the field could be dealt with easily. It was a bit of a puzzle what they were doing there, though, so far from the beach. What eventually stopped work were bones, human bones, and it was the driver who decided that he had had enough rather than the machine.

Irish law concerning antiquities is far stronger than in England, Wales or Scotland. As soon as a site is discovered it is automatically protected and only a licensed archaeologist is subsequently allowed to investigate it. Hugh John knew the law and, startled though he

was, reported his find to Dúchas, the Heritage Service for Ireland. They sent archaeologist Betty O'Brien to investigate. Betty knew before she got there that some of the disturbed graves were possibly edged with slabs of

The beautiful coastline of Donegal Bay, home to an early Christian community.

stone. As an expert on early Christian Ireland, Betty knew that this was a method of burial used in the sixth and seventh centuries AD. As soon as she saw the site Betty realized that her hunch had been correct, but the disturbance was greater than she had feared. Fragments of bone littered the sand among the boulders and already rabbits were digging energetically in the disturbed sand. It was clear that the exposed graves needed to be investigated and the extent of the burial ground defined before any attempts could be made to preserve what remained of this important new site. Dúchas agreed that urgent investigation was required and, in a few weeks, Betty was back with a small team of helpers and the *Meet the Ancestors* team.

It was a long trip to Ballymacaward, just outside the town of Ballyshannon which lies on either side of the River Erne at the place where it runs out into Donegal Bay. The bay is very beautiful and very protective. Mountains rise on either side and long fingers of hard limestone rock jut out from the sandy shoreline. When we arrived, Betty explained that she was very puzzled by the site. There were no previous records of a burial site anywhere nearby, or even any folklore concerning an ancient site. In fact the only recorded use that she had found of the area where the burials were located was as a rabbit warren. Although the location of the cemetery was unusual, in a very marginal position close to the seashore, Betty knew of a very similar site at Inisboffin, 'The Island of the White Cow'. Here there was a church and a freshwater lake and the cemetery lay between the church and the sea. There were some ingredients missing at Ballymacaward but maybe they would turn up later.

By the time we arrived at the excavation Betty's team had cleared away some of the loose sand and were puzzling over the boulders. Rounded and water worn, there were plenty of them on the beach only about 50 metres away, but what were they doing here? As more sand was cleared, the spread of boulders gradually took on a circular shape and the edges of the circle seemed in places to be defined by small upright slabs of stone. What was appearing was evidence of a deliberately built circular pile of boulders, well defined and requiring considerable effort to construct. Betty felt that this was some form of cairn that was probably built on a rock outcrop that had been enhanced with boulders and clay. This cairn was obviously older than the early Christian burials, but how much older?

Little did I realize as I asked Betty if I could help her with the excavation that I would provide one of the first firm clues to the age of the cairn. Betty asked me to trowel over the surface of the sand close to the centre of the cairn where there were no signs of any burials. What were obvious here were the marks made by the teeth of the bulldozer bucket, scoring the firm yellow sand and, in one place, an unexpected patch of something much darker. A quick scrape showed a small circular patch of black soil and within it odd flecks of a hard white substance. I recognized it instantly: it was cremated human bone.

The little patch of black soil I had discovered turned out to be the remains of a small pit which held not only the cremated bones but some of the ashy sand and charcoal from the funeral pyre. Betty knew that a burial of this type could not be of early Christian date; it was more likely to be from the end of the Iron Age, some time around 100 BC. This took us back at least 600 years earlier than we had expected, but was it far enough?

As we shovelled and brushed away more of the drifted sand the extent of the early Christian cemetery became clearer. Ten graves appeared, nearly all lined with stone slabs and consistently aligned in an east–west direction. Some may have been lidded with stone, creating a stone coffin or perhaps the idea of a stone tomb. Close by one of the more badly disturbed stone-lined graves, the top of a skull just peeped through the surface of the sand. This was the next job Betty gave me, finding the edges of the grave and then excavating the skeleton that lay within it. Why did this person not have stone slabs? This was a question I asked myself as I tried to find the edge of the grave, not easy when it has been cut into sand and refilled soon after with exactly the same sand. Archaeologists rely on being able to identify changes in the colour, composition and texture of the soil that they are digging in, but here all I had to go on was texture – the sand at the edge of the grave was just a little bit firmer.

As more of the skull was revealed, Betty decided that the burial was of a woman, and a very distinctive woman at that. Strangely, although her body must have been intact when it was placed in the grave, not all of her skeleton had survived. It seemed as if she had been given one stone slab, a small one placed over her chest, but all this had served to do over the centuries was to destroy all of her ribs and part of her spine. Her arms were intact, lying by her side, but next to them I discovered a strange substance, not bone but almost

LEFT: *In Ireland graves lined with slabs of stone are a sure indication that the burial took place in the early Christian period.*

RIGHT: *The skeleton of the woman from Donegal, lying in the sands which had held her for nearly 1300 years.*

woody in its structure. When I showed some of this to Betty she became more excited than she had been when we found the cremation. Maybe, through some freak of preservation, wood had survived for over 1000 years and we had the first evidence for a plank-lined grave in Ireland. No wonder Betty was so excited.

When the entire skeleton of the woman had been freed from the sand we could see that she had been laid to rest like all the others on the site, with her head to the west. This, and the fact that she had no offerings placed in her grave for the afterlife, was a clear indication that she had been a Christian. There were other hints too of the way in which she had been buried. Her feet were so close together that the

numerous tiny bones could not be separated into left and right foot
and it seemed as if her feet had stuck up, almost as if they had been
hard up against some obstacle. Betty suggested that the real reason
was that she had been buried in a shroud, binding her feet tightly
together. This was yet more proof of Christian burial.

So much seemed to have happened in the week since we had
arrived at Betty's excavation. What was supposed to be a burial site of
one date had turned, through investigation, into something far older
in origin. This is the fascination of archaeology, that ideas constantly
change and the story that unfolds as an excavation progresses is rarely
as straightforward as it first seems!

Wandering around the beach with Betty, we could see clearly the
places where both the boulders and the stone slabs had been collected.
But why had someone chosen that particular place to build the original cairn? Betty now thought it might date back maybe another thousand years, into the Bronze Age. By this time the excavation in the
middle of the cairn had dug through sand to what Betty felt was solid
bedrock. This seemed to confirm her original idea, that the cairn was
built on an outcrop of rock. This may always have been part of the
mainland or possibly, before being engulfed by drifting dune sand,
even a small rocky island in the bay. We needed to find out for certain
as Jane Brayne, our illustrator, was anxious to start her drawing of the
early Christian landscape.

There were two ways to answer the question. One involved a
mechanical digger and some very large holes, the other a geophysical
survey and no more disturbance than a few small probes stuck into the
ground. We chose the geophysical survey. The principle of this
remarkable method of seeing beneath the surface is that different soils
and rocks have varying levels of natural magnetism and will also vary
in their ability to conduct electrical currents. When these natural soils
are disturbed by human activity their magnetic or electrical signature
can be changed and the changes read by sophisticated instruments.
Skilled interpretation of the data produced can identify buried walls,

pits and ditches or, we hoped, would tell us whether solid bedrock lay beneath Betty's cairn.

It is sometimes very easy to become so absorbed in an excavation that you fail to look around and explore its surroundings. But now the geophysical survey had provided a good excuse to leave the site. As Martina McCarthy and her team from Geoarch Surveys set up their probes over the excavation site Jane and I took the opportunity for exploration. The landscape around the burial site has its own mystery. The spot that Jane chose for her vantage point over the burial site lay on one of the low rocky ridges that flank the site on both sides and lead down to the sea where they jut out on to the beach. On this ridge the exposed rocks seem sculpted into strange shapes, piled into unusual structures, their surfaces hollowed into perfect circular basins where rainwater collects. Although this construction and sculpture is the work of natural forces, the erosive power of wind and rain, it still lends magic to the place. Between the ridge and the burial site lies a small lake that we had all noted as we passed by on our way to the excavations. It was only on close inspection that we realized, close to the sea though it lay, that it was fresh water. Frank McGonigle, the farmer's brother, told us more as we sat by its side. Local legend has it that the lake is bottomless, never dries up and that it contains the church plate from the local Abbey of Asseroe, hidden at the time of the Reformation. But to us the most fascinating bit of information that Frank imparted was its name. Locally it was known as Loughna-manfin: 'The Lake of the Fair Women', and we recalled what we had just been told about the burials on site. All of those excavated so far had been of women. Was this just a coincidence or was the name of the lake a long-remembered folk memory of the women buried on the old cairn?

We now had both a burial ground and a freshwater lake, two of the ingredients that the site at Inisboffin possessed. Where was the church though? Once again Betty could provide the answer. Close by inland is a little village called Kilbarron, a name which probably relates to Finbar, an early Irish saint. Betty took us there to see the ruins of a tiny church and explained that although what we could see dated back only to the twelfth century, there had been a church there for many centuries before that. It all seemed to fit into place.

Just before he returned to the farm after telling us the legends of the lake, Frank casually imparted another bit of information. In the field next to the lake, before the hedges were removed and it was levelled for cultivation, there had been a bit of a curved bank, 'like one of those old forts...'. It was wonderful to see Betty's first excited reaction when we passed on Frank's bit of news. She was convinced that what

ABOVE: *The naturally sculpted rocks lent an additional air of mystery to the landscape around the site.*

RIGHT: *'The Lake of the Fair Women' – perhaps the bottomless guardian of an abbey's treasure.*

he had seen must have been part of a ring fort or 'rath', a circular ditched and banked settlement site, the sort of place that you would have lived in if you were well-to-do in early Christian times. We could not believe that we maybe had another part of the jigsaw falling into place – if this settlement was the same date as the burials we were excavating, could the people who were buried on site have lived close by as well? This was obviously the ideal time to have a geophysical survey team on site, a team who could be persuaded to do a little bit more exploration once they had finished the cairn and maybe answer this question as well.

Although the results of geophysical survey often require process-
ing and analysis once instrument readings have been taken in the
field, it can be possible to get a good first impression as soon as the
work is done. Geologist Colm Jordan had also come along to have a
look at the site and he and Martina tried to explain to us what they
thought was happening deep under the burial cairn. Martina's survey
had showed no bedrock, simply deep sand, which meant that our idea
of a rocky promontory or even a small island had to be abandoned. If
what Betty had found was not solid bedrock, then what was it? If it
had been brought to the site from the beach then the original
structure of the cairn must have been far more complex than Betty
could ever have imagined. This seemed like a classic case where the
answer to a question simply raises another set of questions. The 'ring
fort' was no clearer either; there was certainly something in the field
where Frank had seen his curving bank, but the magnetometer had
not given us the clear and unambiguous plan that we had hoped it
would.

At last Jane had all the information that she needed for her landscape and, as she completed her first drawings, it was nearing the time
for us to leave. We had seen the site progress from the simple cemetery that we had all expected to one with a long and complex history
that we were only starting to understand. We had watched as the disturbed burials from early Christian times were excavated and had
helped as one person emerged from the sand. To us she was our 'Lady
of the Sands' and we hoped that she would now start to share with us
the story of her life.

With the excavation completed and the site covered over for protection, it was time to find out more about our 'lady'. The first stop
for her fragile bones was with Maire Delaney, the lecturer in anatomy
at Trinity College Dublin. Before Maire told us about the bones, she
had some bad news. The grave in which our woman had lain had not
been the unique find that we had thought, and the 'plank' that Betty
and I had been so excited about was bone after all. As if this wasn't

enough of a disappointment, we then saw our woman's bones, or rather what had survived the centuries of burial in the sand. There seemed to be far fewer than when I had first exposed them but Maire was still able to paint a picture of a woman and her life. She was slender, perhaps no more than 5ft (1.5 metres) tall, and was aged between thirty-five and forty-five when she died. Although now in several pieces, her skull seemed to have survived fairly well and on it Maire was able to identify two tiny but significant marks. One, on the upper part of her left eye socket, showed where a vein had become enlarged and this, coupled with a thinning of the bone on the inside of the socket, showed that she had suffered from chronic inflammation of the lachrymal gland. This would have caused a painful swelling, together with a sore and slightly drooping eye, and our woman must have had this inflammation for a long time, long enough for it to have caused the tiny changes in her bone that Maire had noticed.

Maire also found the woman's teeth very interesting. Not only did they not show much sign of wear, suggesting that she may have eaten quite a refined diet, but the lack of any build-up of tartar suggested that she had also taken some care with her dental hygiene. There was also a strange worn groove in one of the woman's front teeth, so small that at first it was impossible to see what Maire was pointing out. She felt that it was not damage but the result of wear, some action repeated time after time during the woman's life. Maire's suggestion was that she had been repeatedly drawing threads through her teeth – perhaps this was a clue to her occupation in life? At first we were sceptical; it seemed like quite a nice idea but could it ever be proved?

Far from the intact skeleton which had lain in the Donegal sands, the bones of our woman were now fragmented and crumbling. But they had already yielded some of her life's secrets and they could yield more. Some were to be used for radiocarbon dating, to provide an indication of when she died, but conventional dating, with its thirty- or forty-year margin of error, was not going to be good enough. To be able to link her death with the remarkable historical records that Betty had told us existed for this period in Irish history, we were going to need greater precision. This was why we headed off to Gerry McCormack's laboratory in Belfast. Here Gerry and his team have refined radiocarbon dating to a state where they can obtain a date with an error margin of as little as eighteen years. There is a price, though, as this high-precision dating requires comparatively large samples of wood, charcoal or bone to provide sufficient radioactive carbon. For years, like many archaeologists, I had sent samples to dating laboratories without any clear idea of how they calculated a radiocarbon date for me. Now I could see the whole complicated process from start to finish.

Here goes. In what seemed like a very brutal first stage the majority of our woman's limb bones were crushed so they could be placed in a glass vessel. Here the mineral part of the bones was dissolved in hydrochloric acid, leaving only the organic fraction, a brown jelly-like substance called collagen. After drying, what remained in a foil dish was something that looked like, but certainly didn't smell like, very sticky toffee. This was then placed in a tube with oxygen and nitrogen and burnt at a high temperature, turning it into carbon dioxide. The gas was then cleaned of impurities by bubbling it through a solution of potassium permanganate (a lovely beetroot colour) before any water vapour was removed using dry ice. As someone who never progressed beyond O level general science (Grade D), by this time I was already confused, but the process continued. Lithium metal was melted in a furnace made from a special carbon-free steel and the carbon dioxide was passed over it, resulting in lithium carbide. Water was added to this, resulting in acetylene gas that was then dried and any excess hydrogen and oxygen driven off. Next, the acetylene was turned into benzine by heating it with a catalyst, a stage that Gerry informed me was critical – the wrong temperature and lots could go wrong. If nothing goes wrong it is a simple matter of adding a few drops of phosphorus to the benzine, popping it into a liquid scintillation

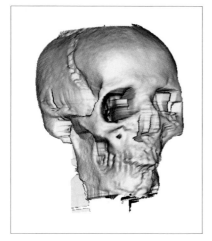

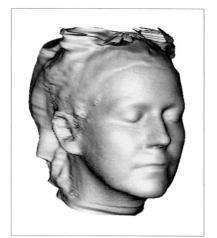

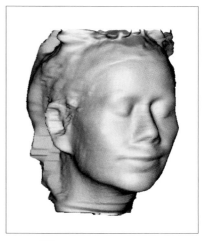

1 *The skull, distorted by centuries of pressure from the overlying sand, was bent back into shape by Robin's computer.*

2 *The 'average' face, created by merging those of a selection of women aged between thirty-five and forty-five years old.*

3 *The distinctive face which emerged when the 'average' face was wrapped over the contours of the ancient skull.*

machine, counting the tiny flashes for a few weeks or months and calculating the date. Simple, really.

Gerry and his team go to extraordinary lengths to refine this process and the precision they achieve probably represents the limits of current technology. Gerry had a simpler description – as far as he was concerned it was just 'a mixture of witchcraft and cookery'.

With the radiocarbon process well under way there were questions which only our woman's skull could answer. After obtaining a temporary export licence we were allowed to bring the fragments to England where they were first consolidated to enable them to be handled without causing any damage. Richard Neave's team was then able to rebuild the fragments into a complete skull. What emerged though was a skull that had been severely distorted by centuries of pressure from the overlying sand and which could not simply be bent back into shape. Fortunately Robin Richards's computer can do things with the data from scanning the skull that could not be done with the now solid bone of the skull itself. The scan showed clearly the direction of the soil pressure which fitted exactly with what we knew of the way the skull had lain in the ground. With this distortion corrected, Robin could proceed with his part of the facial reconstruction.

In the grave our woman's skull had hinted at a very distinctive face, and we were not disappointed. The one that emerged from Robin's computer was very different from the average that he fed in and confirmed what we had felt when we first saw the skull in the ground: that our woman was a person of distinction, at least in her facial features. This was the face that Jane started to paint, this elegant woman from Donegal, but she knew that she would not yet be able to finish it. Until Gerry's laboratory gave us the date of her death we could only guess at the style and detail of her dress, the final bits of the jigsaw that Jane needed.

Seeing the complete skull reminded us of the strange groove in the tooth that Maire had noticed, and her insistence that it was something significant. We were still sceptical and decided to go and see someone who we were sure would be able to give us the definitive answer. David Whittaker of the University of Wales School of Medicine had already demonstrated to us with some of our earlier burials (see Chapters 1 and 5) how he could give an accurate estimate of a person's age from their teeth. This time we had a different question for him, but before he looked at the peculiar groove he did give us an age for our woman. She turned out to be at the older end of the range that Maire had estimated, perhaps between forty-five and fifty when she died, and David confirmed the idea that she had eaten a relatively refined diet. This really emphasized the problems in determining the age of a person from their teeth: the coarser the diet, the more your teeth wear and the older you appear to be. It seemed as if David's method provided the only reliable way in which the teeth could be used for estimating age.

The groove required a different approach, and David decided that high magnification under a scanning electron microscope would pro-

Home to our woman? An early Christian settlement reconstructed at the Ulster History Park.

vide him with the answer. The tooth was first 'sputtered', not as unpleasant as it sounds as it involves coating it in gold. This helps to clarify the microscope image but disappointingly the tooth ended up looking black rather than gold. After experimenting with several different magnifications David settled on x200 and decided that he agreed with Maire – the groove was caused by wear and not by any damage to the tooth. It seemed, at this scale, to be almost thread-shaped and David felt that it might have been the result of something that this woman did repeatedly, perhaps connected with her occupation. The position of the groove, between two of her incisors, was quite a sensible place to hold things, so were we any nearer to her occupation or had we followed this lead as far as it would take us?

We had to return the skull to Dublin, so Betty decided that, as we were back in Ireland, we should pay a visit to the Ulster History

Park. Here there are reconstructions of everything from early prehistoric houses to complete monastic sites, but what we wanted to see was a replica of a rath or ring fort, the sort of early Christian settlement that we had found hints of close to our woman's burial place. Seeing the traces of post holes and filled-in ditches faithfully translated into real structures helps so much to bring the past to life, and the rath was a revelation. Passing through a gated entrance into a circular enclosure, defended by a ditch and a high, palisade-topped bank, we sat inside a cosy circular hut, its walls of woven wood insulated with straw and bracken, its roof of thatch. A fire burned in a central hearth, the smoke curling upward to drift out through the thatch, and around us lay the everyday objects that our woman would have used. I was surprised at the lack of pottery but Betty explained that, in the early Christian period, the Irish didn't make pottery, they cooked in metal cauldrons and ate out of wooden bowls. At the back of the house stood a loom, for weaving flaxen thread, and once again this brought me back to that groove in the tooth. So far we had heard expert opinions from both Maire and David but here we had the opportunity to ask the question to someone who maybe had the same occupation as our woman. Elizabeth Harkin is a weaver and showed us a bundle of flax, prepared ready for spinning and looking uncommonly like a hank of long fine grey hair. Elizabeth explained that Donegal was an important flax-growing area at the time that our woman lived, when the flax was spun using a drop spindle, not a spinning wheel. She also explained that it helps the spinning if the flax is damp and promptly demonstrated this by passing a thin strand of flax through her mouth, hooking it behind her front

Elizabeth the weaver demonstrating the correct way to wet flax.

teeth in exactly the same place as our woman had her groove. I was finally convinced. Our woman had been a flax spinner, spinning the threads that would be woven into fine linen cloth.

At the Ulster History Park we had seen the evidence for life in early Christian Ireland and it was here too that Betty showed us the evidence for what happened at death. We had assumed, from the way in which our woman's bones, particularly her feet, had lain in the grave, that she had been wrapped in a shroud for burial, and Betty had found references to just this practice. There are accounts from AD 597 of the burial on Iona of Columba who was wrapped in 'sindonibus', clean fine linen cloths, and with no

At high magnification under the scanning electron microscope, the groove in the woman's tooth appeared smooth and worn.

mention of a coffin. Betty had brought along some fine linen and, as Bucy McDonald, our researcher, was gently wrapped and finally bound with some linen thread, we all became very aware of the importance of ceremony in the transition from life to death. Was this how our woman had been laid in the sand at Ballymacaward?

Our picture of the 'Lady of the Sands' was growing with each new

For burial, the woman from Donegal would have been tightly shrouded in fine linen, her face covered just before she was lowered into her grave.

piece of evidence, but so much seemed to be resting on the radiocarbon date. It seemed to be an age in coming but, as I had seen at Gerry's laboratory, it was a complex process and could not be rushed. Finally the date was ready and at last we were going to find out exactly when she had lived. Betty was jubilant when Gerry told us the results, justifiably so, as she had been exactly right with her predictions. Our woman had died in the early seventh century, probably between AD 620 and 630, and the cremation burial dated to the later Iron Age, about 700 or 800 years earlier.

Such a precise date gave Jane the clues that she needed to the sort of clothes our woman would have worn. As a Christian her head would have been covered and she would have worn a simple woven dress, edged with a decorative woven strip and secured with a pin. The type of pin is well known, but the finer its craftsmanship and decoration, the higher the wearer's status. Early Irish laws, first written down in the eighth century AD but dating from earlier, actually regulate the type of pins that could be worn and even the direction in which the pin should point.

What was even more exciting was the information contained within the historical records from this time. Their survival is quite remarkable and the area around Ballyshannon is mentioned frequently in early historical and mythological sources written in both Irish and Latin from around AD 650 onwards. The mouth of the River Erne was a popular crossing place in early times and the land around became a much-disputed border area. Armed with the date from our woman's burial, Irish historian Edel Bhreathnach was able to suggest that she might have belonged to one of two rival dynasties, the Cenel Coirpri or the Cenel Conail, both part of a wider confederation known as the Ui Neill. So who was our 'Lady of the Sands'? The final picture was of a middle-aged woman of noble birth, who lived and died at a time when certain dynasties claimed descent from women. She could have been an important matriarch, or was perhaps used to forge a link through marriage between warring groups. She lived over 1300 years ago, maybe in the rath that lies close to the very special lake, 'The Lake of the Fair Women'.

Our lady, with her gentle face and troubled eye, must have been aware that in death, along with the other woman of her dynasty, she would lie in an ancient burial ground with her pagan ancestors. Would this have concerned her? Would she, we wondered, have been aware of the words of the ancient Irish text; 'Christians who are buried among pagans were visited by angels and the angels returned sad'? She may not have known the history of her burial ground but she would have known of its other function. Lay claim to the burial site, by burying in it your own dead, and you could call upon your ancestors to assist with your claim to disputed land.

We said our farewells back at Ballymacaward, in the dunes that line the bay and that had shrouded the ancestral burial ground for so many years. Our Lady of the Sands had shared some of her secrets with us and, one beautiful evening, we re-created her burial, placing a shrouded body (once again played by Bucy, our brave researcher) in a sandy grave, her head to the west as the sun set over the bay.

POSTSCRIPT

Since the end of the excavation and all of the work that went into creating a picture of our lady and her surroundings, we have kept in close touch with Betty and her research. It was with a mixture of excitement and trepidation that we heard she was returning to Ballymacaward for a second season of excavation. Excitement because it was a fascinating site which had clearly not yet given up all of its secrets, trepidation because Betty might find that all of the previous year's ideas were wrong. Such is archaeology.

In the event, Betty found that the site was founded on a rock outcrop but that much of it was buried under about a metre of sand. It appears that the first rocky cairn, smaller in diameter than the one

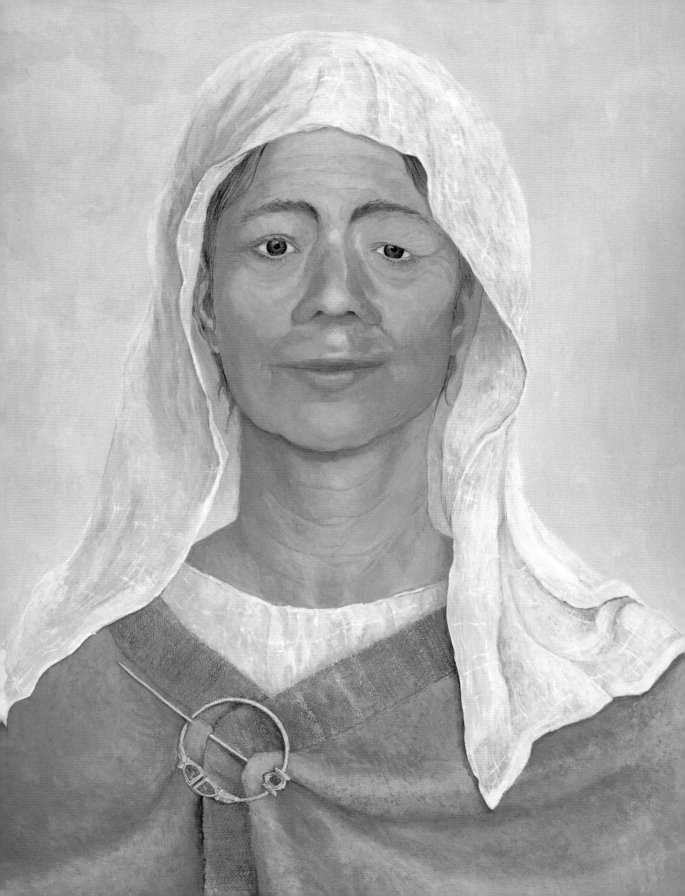

that we saw and about 2 metres high when first built, dates as far back as the Bronze Age, about 1000 BC at the very latest. This was extended in the Iron Age and the cremation burial that we found last year is only one part of a ritual area within which charcoal and cremated bone were scattered widely. Only one more slab-lined grave turned up.

No one thought when those first bones turned up in the Donegal sands that what would eventually be revealed was a place sacred to both pagans and Christians, where ashes and bones would be laid to rest over sixteen centuries.

LEFT: *Close by the shore of Donegal Bay, the 'Lady of the Sands' was laid to rest beside her ancient ancestors.*

ABOVE: *A tranquil scene in the seventh century, but the living disputed the territory with the bones of the dead.*

THE ROSE GARDEN MYSTERY

MALMESBURY IS A small town of warm stone houses and churches, lying at the edge of the Cotswolds in north Wiltshire. Its road signs proudly boast of ancient charters and point the way to a once great Benedictine abbey, the ruins of which still dominate the sleepy streets. Before its destruction in the sixteenth century the Abbey played an important part in the town's history and occasionally, even today, still plays a part in Malmesbury life.

Close to the ruins lies Abbey House, home to Ian and Barbara Pollard and their children. Barbara is a former model and Ian is an architect with a passion for garden design and the Abbey. As its name hints, their house lies quite close to the medieval ruins, in fact part of the Abbey lies within their garden where Ian has laid out borders to show the walls of a long-vanished chapel. But gardening when your garden lies within an ancient monument always has to be carried out with care — the remains may not be very far beneath the surface, as Martin Roberts, the Pollards' gardener, found out one day when he was planting some roses. Ian had a great idea to plant 2000 roses for the millennium, but this meant Martin had a lot of digging to do. He had been warned to look out for a buried water pipe, so he was quite prepared when his spade struck something solid. It was not metal, though; whatever he had hit was made of stone.

At first Martin was not sure exactly what he had found but, as he cleared away the soil with his hands, curiosity turned to amazement and shock as he uncovered a row of human teeth. Suddenly he realized that he had found a coffin and not only that, but it was occupied. Ian and Barbara had lived with the Abbey ever since they moved into their house, but a burial in the rose bed was something they could not have expected. Curiosity got the better of Ian and, with Martin's help, more soil was cleared away until the coffin was fully exposed. They realized that they had better stop when, close to the exposed coffin, the top of a second skull appeared. This one was quite obviously in a simple earth-cut grave, and was hastily covered over again. They were plainly in the middle of a cemetery.

With the top of the stone coffin fully exposed, what now became obvious was not only the fact that it was beautifully constructed, cut from a solid block of stone and with a neat recess at its wider end for the occupant's head, but also its huge size. It was over 7ft (2.1 metres) long — even inside it measured 6ft 4in (1.9 metres) — and, as soon as word of the find leaked out, rumours started to fly round Malmesbury of the giant that had been found in the garden of Abbey House. The speculation about the owner of the teeth that Martin had seen did not stop there either.

Fortunately for the speculators, Malmesbury Abbey could provide a few possible candidates, people of sufficient importance to have been given such a grand burial. The oldest was the first Abbot, St Aldhelm, the legendary worker of miracles who lived in the late seventh century. Or there was the famous Brother Elmer, the flying monk.

Elmer was quite a character who, in the year 1000, decided that he
had worked out a way to fly. So confident was he in his home-made
wings that he donned them and jumped from the tower of the Abbey.
He must nearly have got it right as he flew about 200 metres before
landing and breaking both his legs. Unfortunately we will never
know whether this first test flight would have resulted in improve-
ments and a more successful follow-up as the Pope banned him from
making a second attempt.

> He had by some contrivance fastened wings to his hands and feet in
> order that looking on the fable as true he might fly like Daedalus, and
> collecting the air on the summit of a tower had flown for more than
> the distance of a furlong, but agitated by the violence of the wind and

MAILDVLPHVS   ELMER

the current of air, as well as by the consciousness of his rash attempt, he fell and broke his legs and was lame ever after. He used to relate as the cause of his failure his forgetting to provide himself a tail.

(William of Malmesbury, *History of the Kings of England*)

Perhaps the most tantalizing suggestion was that the coffin was the last resting place of Athelstan, grandson of King Alfred the Great and the first Saxon King of all England. He made Malmesbury his capital in 923 and, as a cultured scholar, built up the Abbey's possessions, endowing it with fine objects and beautiful books. Athelstan's tomb lies in a corner of the Abbey, but it is empty. Popular rumour has it that his bones were removed from this tomb as protection from relic hunters and buried in the Abbot's garden, the garden that now belongs to Ian and Barbara Pollard. There was only one problem with this idea. Athelstan died in 939 and, even without a detailed examination, the coffin in the rose garden looked at least 300 years later. It was clear that the answer lay in the contents of the coffin, but what was to be done with them now?

Strictly speaking, Ian should not have uncovered the coffin as it lay within an ancient monument of national importance where there are clear guidelines about disturbance of the ground. It *was* uncovered, though, as we found when we were invited along to have a first look, and English Heritage had to decide what was to happen next. Amanda Chadburn, the Inspector of Ancient Monuments for Wiltshire, decided that the coffin should stay where it lay, as removing it would cause even more disturbance to the buried remains of the abbey. But what was to happen to the skeleton that lay in the coffin? After much deliberation Amanda decided that it should be properly excavated. The first part of this decision was not well received by Ian and Barbara. Just after it had been discovered the coffin had been an added attraction to an open day in their garden where it had generated huge local interest. So now they were not only curious about the person who was buried in their rose bed, but felt that the coffin ought to be removed and put on local display. This was not the last

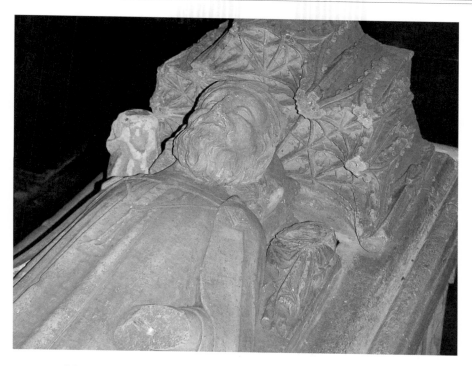

we would hear of the debate between the Pollards and Amanda.

Another candidate for the coffin's occupant? In the Abbey lies the empty tomb of Athelstan, first Saxon King of all England.

English Heritage sent along Jon Humble, one of their Central Archaeological Service team, to carry out the excavation. It was clear from the start that this was going to be only a one-man job, but that I could sit and watch and maybe help with the odd bit of bucket emptying and bone lifting. It was quite strange to start the excavation with a potential cast list already in mind and an awareness of the intense interest of Malmesbury's citizens in our coming up with a suitable occupant for the magnificent coffin.

It didn't take too long to dismiss one of the candidates. As soon as the soil which filled the coffin was removed and the rest of the skeleton exposed, we could state with some confidence that, although it belonged to a man, it was not Athelstan. If it had been the great Saxon king lying in the coffin then his bones, removed from the Abbey many years after he had died, would have been out of their

correct anatomical order, maybe even in a jumbled heap. What did emerge was a complete skeleton, each bone in place and, as more was uncovered, it became obvious that it didn't quite fill the coffin. So, much to our disappointment, we had to admit to Ian and Barbara and the local press that not only had we not found Athelstan but we hadn't found the Malmesbury Giant either. Finally, when the bones were brushed clean to be drawn and photographed, and we were able to carefully examine the leg bones, they were both intact, with no signs of old healed breaks. This ruled out Eilmer the flying monk. We now had an anonymous man and an empty coffin, still in the ground.

With the bones removed, we had the opportunity to examine the coffin more carefully and it became even more obvious what a beautiful piece of craftsmanship it was. It had been hewn from a solid block

LEFT: *The real occupant of the stone coffin: not a giant, not Elmer, and not, to great local disappointment, King Athelstan.*

RIGHT: *The beautifully worked limestone coffin.*

of limestone, quarried either at Malmesbury itself or a few miles away at Tetbury. For a practical assessment of how it would have been made we turned to Tony Finch, aka 'Tone the Stone', self-styled stonemason of the parish. Tony explained to us, in his own inimitable way, that the shaping of the coffin and the hollowing out, even of the beautifully shaped head recess, would have been done not with a hammer and chisel but with an axe. His explanation was so enthusiastically illustrated with sweeping gestures of appropriate stone-working tools that we feared for the safety of the stonework. It was a convincing demonstration, though, and concluded with Tony's confident assertion that whoever made it was right-handed. As we stood and gazed at the coffin the discussion turned to how long it would take to make it, allowing for the transport of the rough block of stone from the quarry. Tony reckoned that it would be nearly a month, which helped to explain why the coffin was too big for its occupant. Coffins like this must have been available from a stonemason as and when they were required, for the burial ceremony could certainly not wait for a month while one was specially prepared. Whoever lay in this coffin was not a giant; they had just been given an oversized resting place, the next one available off the shelf.

Having convincingly eliminated all the previously suggested characters, there was a certain amount of pressure on us to suggest an alternative. The first clues to the identity of the man in the flowerbed were going to come from the coffin itself, and also the place where it lay. Despite Tony's nonchalant assertion that it was a fairly ordinary piece of stonework, the coffin must have belonged to someone of high status, but were they connected to the Abbey? The position of the coffin in the Pollards' garden at first seemed quite a long way from the Abbey ruins, but what survives today is just a fraction of what stood before Henry VIII dissolved the monasteries in 1539. Standing by the present parish church, formed out of the six surviving bays of the original nave of the Abbey, it is hard to grasp the scale of the build-

Malmesbury's parish church is built into the ruins of the Abbey and by its south doorway lies another ancient stone coffin.

ing at the height of its splendour. The nave and the choir together were 86 metres long, with the Lady Chapel adding another 12.5 metres. The building was 32 metres wide and was capped by a spire reputedly taller than that of Salisbury Cathedral. Unfortunately this fell in a storm towards the end of the fifteenth century, demolishing much of the east end of the Abbey in the process, so Henry VIII cannot be held entirely responsible for the state of the Abbey today.

The monk's grave, shown as a roofed tomb, lay close to the north wall of the long-vanished Lady Chapel.

Despite being only one-third of the original building, the present parish church is still an impressive site, crown-

ing the low hill on which Malmesbury lies and visible for miles around. Replace all the missing bits, the results of centuries of neglect, re-use, natural disaster and deliberate demolition, and the position of the newly discovered coffin suddenly becomes clear. We realized that it lay immediately outside the north wall of the long-vanished Lady Chapel, immediately adjacent to a large supporting buttress. This position seemed to suggest that the burial had taken place after the chapel was built in about 1267. Did this location mean that the man was a monk, and the grand coffin that he was quite a senior one? One thing was clear: he wasn't an abbot or prior, for if he had been then he would almost certainly have been buried inside the chapel or the church itself. If we wanted to find out more about this mysterious man, it was clear that we would have to look to see what clues his well-preserved bones could provide.

Because the excavation had been carried out by English Heritage archaeologists the skeleton was to be examined by Simon Mays, whom we had already met when he examined the bones from Bleadon. The picture that emerged was of a man aged about fifty, well-built and quite tall by medieval standards at about 5ft 10in (1.77 metres). Although, as with the majority of people from the past whose remains are examined, there was no sign of what had caused his death, it was clear that he must have suffered some pain particularly during the later years of his life. His teeth were in a terrible state, with problems leading to a badly abscessed jaw, and he suffered from an inflamed toe on his left foot that may have caused him to walk with a slight limp. Simon was able to identify this problem from the formation of new bone on one of our man's toes and at first thought that he might have suffered from leprosy. Looking closely at the skull, Simon could find no other signs of this dreadful disease and concluded that our man must simply have suffered from a localized infection. Despite these problems his overall health appeared to have been good, especially when compared to that of the average medieval peasant. Simon has examined hundreds of skeletons from the cemetery of Wharram Percy, a deserted medieval village in Yorkshire, and could give first-hand evidence of the lives of the villagers. Many children died shortly after birth and those who survived into infancy, ravaged by hunger and disease, often suffered stunted growth. The adults also showed problems caused by nutritional deficiencies and many suffered from acute sinusitis caused by smoky living conditions. The killer disease TB was rife, an unfortunate consequence of sharing dwellings with their beasts, and osteoporosis was just as common centuries ago as it is today.

If this was the pattern of life for the medieval poor, did the bones of our man show a different picture? Was he perhaps a monk, leading a sheltered and privileged life? Simon thought that this was stretching the evidence a little further than he would be prepared to. He also pointed out that, even if he had been a monk and had ended up comparatively well fed and healthy, he had not always been so lucky. X-rays of his leg bones revealed thin white lines, looking at first like regular cracks, running across the whole width of the bone. These are called Harris lines, formed when bone growth stops and then restarts, usually due to starvation or episodes of illness or trauma. Their position relative to the ends of long bones in the arms and legs can also be used to calculate when in life they occurred. These lines showed that, as a boy, our man's growth stopped five times between the ages of four and nine. Most of the intervals between the lines, of 0.5 years, 2.1 years, 1.1 years and 0.9 years, could have taken place at approximately the same time of year, perhaps indicating food shortage in late winter or a seasonal disease. Winter could mean respiratory disease, summer could mean recurring infections. Our man may have ended up well fed but as a child perhaps knew illness, hardship and even starvation.

So far we had a picture of a man aged about fifty years old, whose life in middle age seemed to contrast with his childhood. The position of his burial seemed to suggest that he was a high-ranking monk, but we felt that we needed more confirmation before Jane Brayne could paint his portrait. Robin Richards had used his computer and a data bank of fifty-year-old male faces to create a likeness from the well-preserved skull. The face was very distinctive — 'strong' was a word used by many who saw it — and had a crooked nose and sunken cheeks, all features of the original skull; but should Jane show the tonsured head of a monk or not? There was one more piece of evidence that would finally convince us that our suspicions were correct, and it came from an unlikely source. A tiny sample of one of the man's leg bones had been sent to the Oxford Accelerator for radiocarbon dating. The date that came back was a bit of a disappointment, lying somewhere in the early to middle part of the thirteenth century. This fitted in well with the construction of the Lady Chapel, but it was not precise enough to enable us to search back through the Abbey's records and perhaps identify the individual.

What did emerge from the dating process, though, was some fascinating evidence about our man's diet. Just as with Bleadon Man (pages 60–61), the laboratory could establish whether his food was marine or land-based. In the case of our man, despite the fact that he ended his days in landlocked Malmesbury, a considerable distance from the nearest sea, the evidence suggested that a high proportion of the protein in his diet, perhaps as much as a half, came from sea fish. This new evidence fitted well with results obtained from a known monastic cemetery in York and suggested that our man may have eaten the rigid diet of a medieval monk. The Benedictine rule forbade the eating of meat, except by the sick, although it became common in the thirteenth century for monks to have meat as a treat when dining with the abbot or in the infirmary regardless of whether or not you were ill. Fish was an acceptable substitute for meat and medieval documents record the purchase of considerable quantities of sea fish by monasteries that lay well inland. Herring appeared to be the favourite. One side effect of eating fish is supposed to be the prevention of tooth decay but, judging by the state of our man's teeth, it had not helped him much.

All the evidence pointed towards the man in the stone coffin being a monk, so we felt that Jane could complete her portrait and

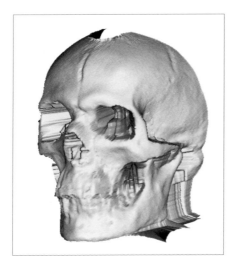

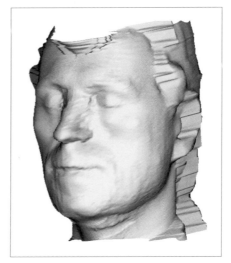

The monk's bones told a story of childhood poverty and adult plenty; his skull showed the pain of toothache.

Like a death mask, the computer-generated face has form but no life and requires artistry to open its eyes.

show the man as a Benedictine. This order wore a full-length gown with full sleeves, belted at the waist and sometimes with a hood. The gown would have been of natural coloured wool, mottled grey or brown, but over this they wore a loose black-hooded scapula, the monk's 'habit', and a black cape for outdoors. It was these outer garments that gave the Benedictines the name of 'Black Friars'. Our monk would also have worn some form of sock-like leg covering, and on his feet 'caligae', sandal-like boots similar to those worn by Roman soldiers centuries before.

We felt by this time that we had really discovered a person, but we were curious about the life that he might have led in Malmesbury over 700 years ago. Fortunately the lives of medieval monks are well ordered and documented so we were able to reconstruct his way of life in considerable detail. Most medieval abbeys followed a set of rules laid down in the sixth century by St Benedict, rules which described a simple community in which monks lived together in what amounted to a large

The Malmesbury monk: the calm strength of a thirteenth-century Benedictine.

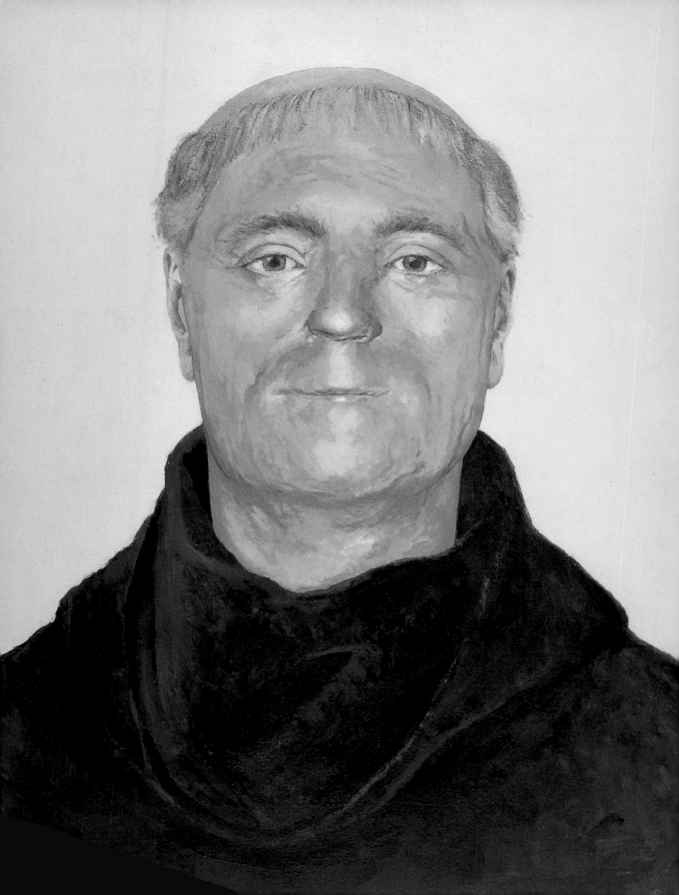

extended family. Even in such an spiritual community, though, a hierarchy inevitably developed, headed by the abbot and closely followed by the 'obedientiaries'. These were senior monks who held powerful posts in the running of the abbey and whose duties allowed them to go outside the abbey and even to miss church services. The almoner distributed charity to the poor, the infirmarer looked after the sick-house, the chamberlain was responsible for all the monks' clothing and also supervised bedding, bathing and shaving. Perhaps the most powerful figure was the cellarer, who managed the purchase of all food and drink. As a guide to monastic life written by Lanfranc, the Archbishop of Canterbury, describes him, 'He should be the father of the whole community and should have a care for the sound and still more for the sick.' Perhaps our monk was one of the 'obedientiaries', maybe the cellarer, providing for his fellow monks a comfortable life that was a far cry from his own childhood.

Whatever his rank within the monastic community, the day for our monk would have been filled with a strict regime of prayer, starting with Matins at about two o'clock in the morning and ending with Compline at about seven o'clock in the evening. There were other regulations too. The rule of St Benedict discouraged unnecessary conversation and, in the refectory where meals were taken, a rule of silence generally applied. Ritual washing took place daily but bathing was less frequent and, from instructions provided in the eleventh century, was obviously not meant to be enjoyed.

The life of a monk was austere and, from a modern perspective, it is difficult to see what drew recruits. From the time of St Benedict until the twelfth century one of the major sources was children, pledged to the monastic life by their parents, and young adults who chose to enter a monastery. Perhaps our monk, whose childhood seemed to be marked by hardship and even starvation, was pledged by his parents as a way of making sure that he would be well fed and cared for. If he did start his life in poverty then he appears to have ended it shielded from the hardships of medieval life.

Given the regulations that governed medieval monastic life, it is not surprising that death and burial involved ceremonies carefully laid down and unchanged for centuries. At the first signs of mortal sickness our monk would have been taken to the infirmary (by a strange irony now Ian and Barbara's house), where he would have received the Last Rites. Here too, when he had 'yealded the ghoste', the first part of the burial ritual, the Commendation of the Soul, was carried out. Before his final burial in the stone coffin, his body was placed in a temporary one of wood and carried to the Abbey church. Here he lay, before the high altar, his feet pointing to the east as they soon would be in the ground. Candles burned around his pall-draped coffin and close by his fellow Benedictines carried out an all-night vigil. At dawn, dressed only in coarse hair shirt, he would have been carried in procession to a favoured plot next to the Abbey's Lady Chapel and laid to rest in the fine stone coffin. Here he lay for over 700 years until Martin's spade first disturbed that rest.

In the end Ian and Barbara failed to come up with a solution for displaying the coffin on the ground which satisfied English Heritage, and Amanda insisted that it was protected and reburied. Meanwhile, despite all the scientific evidence, speculation about the identity of the monk still carries on. A new candidate, the historian William of Malmesbury, has recently entered the arena, despite having died nearly 100 years before the time that radiocarbon dating indicates that our monk died. But what became of him? Many of us who saw him emerge from the ground, and were involved as his bones yielded up their secrets, felt that we had come to know a real person. For us there could only be one final resting place for those bones, back in the coffin where they had lain for so many years. But they are not there: the coffin is empty and the bones lie in a cardboard box on a shelf in a local museum. To me this should not have been his final resting place and I said my personal farewell to the monk of Malmesbury in the Pollards' garden, at the place where we had first met, as once again the rose garden shrouded its own medieval mystery.

CHRONOLOGY

THE NINE ANCESTOR sites that we investigated spanned nearly 4000 years, from the Neolithic period in prehistoric times to the Middle Ages. The chronology places each of the ancestors in their own period and gives a summary of major events. In prehistoric times, before written records exist, our understanding of chronology is largely based on radiocarbon dating. With very few precise dates, what can be suggested are broad date ranges for the periods that are used to divide up the prehistoric past. Written history begins with the Roman invasions of AD 43 and from here on most major events can be assigned to more precise dates.

THE YEARS BC
PREHISTORY

MESOLITHIC

c.10,000 The end of the last Ice Age when mainland Britain was still joined to the continent by a land bridge and was populated by mobile groups of hunters and gatherers using tools of stone and bone. This is known as the 'Mesolithic' or Middle Stone Age period.

c.7000 The English Channel was finally flooded; Britain was an island from this time onwards but was still covered in dense forest.

NEOLITHIC

c.4000 The beginning of the 'Neolithic' or New Stone Age period, marked by the introduction, at first on a small scale, of farming. Simple forms of wheat are grown and domesticated cattle and pigs are raised. This means that some of the natural woodland is cleared, felled with new types of polished stone and flint axes, and people start to live in more settled communities. The first pottery is produced at this time and groups of people gather together to build structures of stone and earth. These can be for burial (long mounds or 'barrows' which often contain the bones of many people) or for ceremony (hilltop 'causewayed' enclosures such as Windmill Hill in Wiltshire).

c.3000 In the later part of the Neolithic period pottery is now elaborately decorated and new types of ceremonial sites are built, some on a massive scale such as Silbury Hill in Wiltshire. 'Henges' like Stonehenge and Avebury, stone circles and other unusual but related sites can be found from Dorset to Orkney. Long barrows are still used for burial although round barrows, often covering only a single burial, are now starting to be built. *Burial of the woman and children from Cranborne (Chapter 1).*

c.2300 The arrival from mainland Europe of a new finely decorated type of pottery, the 'Beaker', part of a package of new objects including copper weapons and archery equipment. Whether or not these objects are simply imported or are brought in by 'Beaker Folk' is still uncertain. The burial of a single person, often with grave goods, beneath a round barrow, becomes more common. Woodland clearance continues and the lowland landscape becomes more grassy, grazed by sheep.

BRONZE AGE

c.2000 The beginning of the Bronze Age proper, when bronze becomes more widely available for tools and weapons. Single inhumations or cremations under a variety of types of round barrow continue, some with very rich grave goods.
Burial of 'Adam' from Cranborne (Chapter 1).

c.1500 In the middle of the Bronze Age the climate begins to deteriorate and there is the first evidence for both extensive arable farming and the formal division of the landscape. Herders are turning into arable farmers.

IRON AGE

c.800 The Iron Age, marked by the introduction of a new and more functional metal for both weapons and tools. From the earliest part of this period the processes of land division continue and large defended settlements are built, culminating in the sometimes massive hillforts of the later Iron Age. Tribal identity develops during this period, with recognized centres of administration and kings who issue coinage based on that of the Roman Empire. At this time both cremation and inhumation are practised.
Burial of Bleadon Man (Chapter 2).

55 and 54 Exploratory invasions by Julius Caesar and Roman legions. Some southern kingdoms are now under Roman patronage and there is much trade with the Empire.

THE YEARS AD
HISTORY

ROMAN

43 The end of a culturally and spiritually rich prehistory that shaped the face of the British Isles is marked by the Roman invasion under the Emperor Claudius. This is the beginning of four centuries of Roman occupation, perhaps not the start of our civilization as some would have us believe. The military campaigns were followed by the creation of an administrative infrastructure including roads and towns. A formal money economy was now widely adopted. Disposal of the dead was by means of cremation.

60-1 Rebellion of Boudicca – London burned.

70 The foundation of 'Venta Belgarum', Roman Winchester (*Chapter 4*).

122 Emperor Hadrian visits Britain and orders the construction of a wall from the Tyne to the Solway to mark the northern limit of the Empire. The wall eventually becomes a major military frontier.

208-11 The Emperor Septimius Severus resides in Britain and dies at York. Burial rite changes from cremation to inhumation.

c.275-85 Construction of coastal forts from the Wash to Portsmouth.

306 Constantine declared emperor by the British garrison at York. Baptized on his death bed, he was the first emperor to embrace Christianity, which then became the official religion of Roman Britain. Worship of the old gods continued, though churches

and east–west burials without grave goods provide increasing evidence of Christianity *(Chapters 3, 4, 5)*.

c.320 *Burial of Winchester Man (Chapter 4).*

391 Emperor Theodosius issues edict forbidding access to pagan shrines and temples. Archaeological evidence from Britain makes it clear that this measure was not applied with any vigour.

407 Withdrawal of most of the Roman army to fight in Gaul and Spain.

409 The Emperor Honorius failed to appoint new governors to the provinces and tells the cities of Britain that they must defend themselves. This marks the effective abandonment of Britain by the Roman Empire, although contact with the Roman world, largely by Church officials, continues at least until the middle of the fifth century.

ANGLO-SAXON ('DARK AGES')

c.420–50 Fragmentation of the Roman Province. The centuries immediately following the end of Roman rule are often referred to as the 'Dark Ages'. In western Britain many Roman institutions may survive for another century or more, while in the east Anglo-Saxon type settlements and cemeteries become increasingly common *(Chapters 6, 7)*.

432 Traditional date for the arrival of St Patrick in Ireland *(Chapter 8)*.

447–50 Angles settle in Britain from Europe, together with Saxons and Jutes.

c.520 First nunnery in Ireland founded by St Brigid.

550 St David takes Christianity to Wales.

c.550–600 By the later sixth century a number of

Anglo-Saxon kingdoms are starting to form; these include Wessex, Kent and East Anglia. By the early seventh century Mercia and Northumbria become established as major units *(Chapter 9)*.

563 St Columba founds Iona monastery and begins conversion of the Picts.

597 Mission of St Augustine to Britain. Conversion of King Ethelbert of Kent to Christianity.

c.600 *Burial of the Lakenheath Warrior (Chapter 6).*

622–9 Ship burial, possibly of Raedwald, King of the East Anglians, at Sutton Hoo *(Chapter 6)*.

c.620–30 *Burial of the woman from Donegal (Chapter 8).*

660 Appointment of first Bishop of Winchester.

675 St Aldhelm, first Abbot of Malmesbury, writes Latin prose and poetry *(Chapter 9)*.

698 Start of Lindisfarne Gospels.

c.700 Anglo-Saxon poem *Beowulf* composed.

731 The Venerable Bede completes *Ecclesiastical History of the English People*.

736 King Ethelbald of Mercia now styled 'King of Britain'.

784 Offa starts to build Offa's Dyke, defining English/Welsh border.

793 Viking raids start.

851 Danish raids start.

871 King Alfred crowned.

923 Athelstan becomes the first King of all England and makes Malmesbury his capital *(Chapter 9)*.

939 Death of Athelstan and rebuilding of Malmesbury Abbey *(Chapter 9)*.

c.1000 Elmer's flight from the tower of Malmesbury Abbey *(Chapter 9)*.

1012 Danes sack Canterbury.

MEDIEVAL
1066 King Harold II crowned; Norman invasion under William the Conqueror.

1089 Domesday survey completed.

1215 King John signs Magna Carta.

c.1220–60 **Burial of the monk from Malmesbury** *(Chapter 9)*.

1338–1453 Hundred Years' War.

1348–49 Black Death decimates population.

1529 Henry VIII breaks with Rome and dissolves the monasteries *(Chapter 9)*.

ADDITIONAL INFORMATION

I HOPE THAT you have enjoyed hearing about some of our ancestors. Do you want to know more? There are ways that anyone can find out more about the past, by exploring the sites themselves and also museums and places where records are kept.

Different people and organizations can help you to find out about the archaeology in your area but it helps to know the way in which archaeology is organized.

In most of Great Britain each county or district has an archaeological curator. This person is usually based in the Planning Department of the local authority and is responsible for documenting and safeguarding the archaeology in their area. They monitor planning applications and, where one will have an effect on an archaeological site, or an area that may be of significance, suggest appropriate responses. These can vary from insisting on the preservation of important sites, to ensuring that excavations are carried out where necessary. The curator will also usually hold and maintain a record of all archaeological sites in their area, from major castles and abbeys to the find spots of a single coin or fragment of pottery. This is the Sites and Monuments Record (SMR for short) and these records are available to anyone with a genuine interest.

Apart from these more local records there is a National Monuments Record (NMR) housed in Swindon where it is possible to examine aerial photographs, records of historic and listed buildings, and a national record of archaeological sites of all types.

NATIONAL MONUMENTS RECORD
Kemble Drive
Swindon SN2 2GZ
Tel. 01793 414600

The people or organizations who carry out the field-work or excavation specified by archaeological curators are known as contractors. They can be single operators or small groups through to large regional or national 'units'. All need to be approved by archaeology's professional organization, the Institute of Field Archaeologists (IFA). Although most contract archaeology is now carried out at high speed and during the working week, your local archaeological contractor may carry out excavations, fieldwork or activities such as finds washing in which volunteers can participate.

The final resting place for any finds, and the notes, plans and photographs that accompany them, will be an appropriate (usually local) museum. Many museums have archaeologists and will have archaeological material on display. They are also a good place to start and to ask about other local organizations. If you have never been to your local museum, then pay it a visit, have a look at what is on display and find out about other organizations such as local or county societies that organize lectures or field trips. It is best to phone the museum before planning a visit to find out about opening times and also if any special events are planned.

There are also some national archaeological organizations such as:

ENGLISH HERITAGE
23 Savile Row
London W1X 1AB
Tel. 0171 973 3000

English Heritage cares for some of England's most important monuments such as Stonehenge, Hadrian's Wall and Dover Castle. Many of these are open to the public and English Heritage is committed to public education and enjoyment of their sites. Many of them play host to special events such as battles, ceremonies or re-enactments of everyday life. You can contact your local English Heritage site or regional office (phone the London number for details) and they will help you to find out what is going on.

English Heritage also has an Education Service which can provide information about free educational site visits and details of publications, videos and other resources.

ENGLISH HERITAGE EDUCATION SERVICE
Portland House
Stag Place
London SW1E 5EE
Tel. 0171 973 3442

The equivalent organization in Scotland is Historic Scotland which produces a very useful leaflet called *Archaeological Information and Advice*. This can be obtained free from:

HISTORIC SCOTLAND
Longmore House
Salisbury Place
Edinburgh EH9 1SH
Tel. 0131 668 8600

In Wales archaeology is the responsibility of CADW who are based at:

CADW
Crown Building
Cathays Park
Cardiff CF1 3NQ
Tel. 01222 500200

In Ireland the organizations to contact are:

DÚCHAS HERITAGE SERVICE
51 St Stephen's Green
Dublin 2
Tel. 003 531 661 3111

or:

THE ENVIRONMENT OF HERITAGE SERVICES
Department of the Environment of Northern Ireland
5–13 Hill Street
Belfast BT1 2LA
Tel. 01232 235000

A very good way to become involved in archaeology is to join the Council for British Archaeology (CBA). The Council publishes a magazine called *British Archaeology* which provides an excellent round-up of news, articles, reviews and campaigns. There is also a network of regional CBA groups which, among other activities, hold meetings and publish their own newsletters.

The CBA and English Heritage jointly publish *The Archaeology Resource Book*. This provides listings of archaeological organizations and museums and outlines the role of archaeology in education.

The CBA also provides a club for young people aged from 9 to 16. The Young Archaeologists' Club (YAC) issues a lively quarterly magazine, *Young Archaeologist*, giving details of club activities. There are local and regional groups all over the country and if there isn't one near you then ask why! The CBA and YAC are at:

Bowes Morrell House
111 Walmgate
York YO1 9WA
Tel. 01904 671417

A good way of keeping up with what is going on in the world of archaeology is to subscribe to *Current Archaeology*. This is a well-illustrated magazine, published six times a year, that reviews new sites, finds, ideas and books and has a lively letters page.

CURRENT ARCHAEOLOGY
9 Nassington Road
London NW3 2TX
Tel. 0171 435 7517

On a general note about books, those in the series produced by Batsford in association with English Heritage are good, well-illustrated guides to particular sites, regions, periods or topics. (The paperback editions are usually around £15.)

Shire Publications' *Discovery* series are small, reasonably priced, readable paperbacks and provide a good introduction to a wide range of topics.

If you are fascinated by images from the past then read *Making Faces* by John Prag and Richard Neave (British Museum Press, 1997).

THE ANCESTOR SITES

CHAPTER 1
CRANBORNE CHASE

The site, which lies on private land, is now reburied but it does lie in the middle of Cranborne Chase, a wonderful landscape in which some prehistoric sites can be visited including parts of the Cursus. Close by, at the village of Knowlton, is a well-preserved henge inside which lies the ruins of a medieval church. Knowlton lies on the B3078 about 15 miles north of Poole and Bournemouth.

On the outskirts of Dorchester, the county town of Dorset, is Maumbury Rings, another henge that survives well and has free public access. Maumbury had a chequered subsequent history as a Roman amphitheatre and a Civil War gun battery. When in Dorchester it is worth visiting the County Museum with its new archaeology gallery.

DORSET COUNTY MUSEUM
High West Street
Dorchester
Dorset DT1 1XA
Tel. 01305 262735

Cranborne Chase is the area explored by the pioneering archaeologist General Pitt Rivers. There is a gallery devoted to his life and work in Salisbury Museum.

SALISBURY AND SOUTH WILTSHIRE
MUSEUM
The King's House
65 The Close
Salisbury
Wiltshire SP1 2EN
Tel. 01722 332151

For further reading try *Bronze Age Britain* by Mike Parker-Pearson (English Heritage/Batsford, 1993). Despite its title this book does not restrict itself to the Bronze Age but gives a good introduction to the preceding Neolithic period as well.

CHAPTER 2
BLEADON

The Bleadon site is now built over but if you want to find out more about the Iron Age then there are books to read and sites to visit. A good introduction is *Iron Age Britain*, by Barry Cunliffe (English Heritage/Batsford, 1995). Bleadon is close to Weston-super-Mare where the Time Machine Museum has displays of Iron Age finds from the nearby hillfort of Worlebury.

TIME MACHINE MUSEUM
Burlington Street
Weston-super-Mare
North Somerset BS23 1PR
Tel. 01934 621028

Worlebury Hillfort lies on the northern edge of Weston. It is council-owned and well signposted.

The Museum of the Iron Age is located in the:

ANDOVER MUSEUM
6 Church Close
Andover
Hampshire SP10 1DP
Tel. 01264 366283

Any visit here should be combined with a trip to Danebury Hillfort, well signposted off the A343 Salisbury to Andover road and open all year round.

For a reconstruction of life in the Iron Age why not visit the Butser Ancient Farm (also in Hampshire)? This experimental establishment, where long-term studies of ancient farming methods are carried out, has a public area where you can see Iron Age houses, crops and animals. They are also building a Roman villa.

BUTSER ANCIENT FARM
Nexus House
South Gravel Hill
Norndean
Hampshire PO8 0QE
Tel. 01705 598838

Located just off the A3, 5 miles south of Petersfield, 7 miles north of Portsmouth. Open from Easter to October.

CHAPTER 3
MANGOTSFIELD

The site is now built over but if you want to find out more about Roman Britain then there are good books to read and lots of sites and museums to visit.

A good introduction is *Life in Roman Britain*, by Joan Alcock (English Heritage/Batsford, 1996).

Museums that are well worth a visit include:

ROMAN BATHS MUSEUM
Stall Street
Bath BA1 1LZ
Tel. 01225 477785

The Roman bath excavations are displayed here in their original setting.

CORINIUM MUSEUM
Park Street
Cirencester
Gloucestershire GL7 2BX
Tel. 01285 655611

This houses an important Roman collection, including mosaics. While in this area it is worth visiting:

CHEDWORTH ROMAN VILLA
Chedworth
Yanworth
Cheltenham
Gloucestershire GL54 3LJ
Tel. 01242 899256

CHAPTER 4
WINCHESTER

The site is now built over but Winchester is well worth a visit. There is an excellent new Roman gallery in the museum:

WINCHESTER CITY MUSEUM
The Square
Winchester
Hampshire SO23 7DW
Tel. 01962 848269

The Museum Service also publish a very good illustrated souvenir guide called *Venta Belgarum, the Roman Town of Winchester*. Or for more detail see *Winchester* by Tom James in the English Heritage/Batsford series.

Not too far away on the coast in Sussex is the magnificent Roman palace of Fishbourne, well worth a visit to see the luxury in which it was possible to live at this time.

FISHBOURNE ROMAN PALACE
Salt Hill Road
Fishbourne
Chichester
West Sussex PO19 3QR
Tel. 01243 785 859

On a slightly less grand scale is:

ROCKBOURNE ROMAN VILLA
Rockbourne
Fordingbridge
Hampshire SP6 3PG
Tel. 01725 518541

For some idea of the scale and layout of a Roman town, visit one that has never been built over. Silchester lies between Reading and Basingstoke and has surviving walls, a town trail, amphitheatre and lots of information.

CHAPTER 5
SEDBERGH

The cave with its wolf bones and burials is now closed and will not be reopened. Displays of Bronze Age artefacts can be seen at:

THE TULLIE HOUSE MUSEUM,
Castle Street
Carlisle
Cumbria CA3 8TP
Tel. 01228 534781

In the north of England, why not visit Hadrian's Wall or any of its many forts? Look out for appearances of the Ermine Street Guard, the Roman Army at its fiercest and most authentic best.

CHAPTER 6

LAKENHEATH

The site lies within a restricted area and is now built over. There are two museums which have good collections of Anglo-Saxon finds.

IPSWICH MUSEUM AND ART GALLERY
High Street
Ipswich
Suffolk IP1 3QH
Tel. 01473 213761

MOYSES HALL MUSEUM
Cornhill
Bury St Edmunds
Suffolk IP33 1DX
Tel. 01284 757488

There is also an excellent reconstructed Anglo-Saxon village at West Stow which has a major new heritage centre opening in 1999. This will house a new exhibition of Anglo-Saxon finds from Suffolk and is intended to offer the complete Saxon experience. Well worth a visit.

THE VISITORS CENTRE
West Stow Country Park
Icklingham Road
West Stow
Suffolk IP28 6HG
Tel. 01284 728718

While in East Anglia, why not visit Flag Fen, the spectacular site in the Fens providing great insight into Bronze Age life and beliefs? There is a visitor centre and excavations are often being carried out. It is located in Peterborough's Eastern Industrial Area, clearly signed from the Peterborough Ring Road.

FLAG FEN BRONZE AGE EXCAVATION
4th Drove
Fengate
Peterborough
Cambridgeshire PE1 5UR
Tel. 01733 313414
Recommended reading: *Flag Fen, Prehistoric Fen-*
land Centre by Francis Pryor (English Heritage/Batsford 1991).

CHAPTER 7

WINTERBOURNE GUNNER

The site is on private land and is now built over. Finds from the original excavations and from the excavations of other Saxon cemeteries in south Wiltshire are on display in Salisbury Museum (see Chapter 1 for details).

While in Wiltshire it is also worth visiting the Devizes museum in the north of the county. The museum has displays of the spectacular finds from nineteenth-century barrow burial excavations in Wiltshire.

WILTSHIRE ARCHAEOLOGICAL AND
NATURAL HISTORY MUSEUM
41 Long Street
Devizes
Wiltshire SN10 1NS
Tel. 01380 727369

As a good general guide to this period read *Anglo-Saxon England* by Martin Welch (English Heritage/ Batsford 1992)

CHAPTER 8

DONEGAL

The site is now covered over and lies on private land, but Ireland has a rich early Christian heritage and there are many sites to visit. A good overall introduction is provided by *The Archaeology of Early Medieval Ireland* by Nancy Edwards (Batsford, 1996).

A guide to sites to visit can be found in *Guide to National and Historic Monuments of Ireland* by Peter Harbison (Gill and Macmillan, 1992)

The National Museum of Ireland in Dublin is an essential visit:

NATIONAL MUSEUM OF IRELAND
Kildare Street
Dublin 2
Tel. 003 531 677 7444

The Ulster History Park has authentic reconstructions of early Christian settlements and monastic sites among its prehistoric tombs and hunters' camp.

THE ULSTER HISTORY PARK
Cullion
Omagh
Co Tyrone
Northern Ireland BT79 7SU
Tel. 01662 648188

CHAPTER 9

MALMESBURY

Although the site of the burial lies in a private garden you can still visit the Abbey church and the ruins of the other Abbey buildings.

There are two good books in the Batsford/English Heritage series: *Abbeys and Priories* by Glen Coppack (1991) and *Know the Landscape: Monasteries* by Mick Aston.

Among the properties cared for by English Heritage and other conservation organizations are the ruins of many of the great and powerful monasteries that exerted such wealth and power until the Dissolution. These ruins, far more than any museum display, provide a picture of monastic life.

Finally, if you have enjoyed being involved in our investigations, why not try to trace your own ancestors? It is quite fascinating but, be warned, it can become addictive. There are many books on how to do this but, for a start, try *Ancestral Voices: The Complete Guide to British Genealogy and Family History* by Mark D. Herber (Sutton Publishing, 1997).

If you are going to visit any of the areas in which the ancestor sites lie then it is worth investing in the appropriate OS map, 1:50,000 Landrangers are the best. These will give you clear indications of rights of way and of which sites can be visited.

Enjoy your exploration and remember, if you want to know something, ask!

INDEX

ACKNOWLEDGEMENTS

We could not have made *Meet the Ancestors* during 1997 and 1998 without the enthusiastic co-operation of a huge number of archaeologists and scientists who opened up their excavations and their laboratories to our production team. On site our thanks must go not only to the directors and supervisors, but also to the site workers, the 'diggers' who happily, on occasions, cleaned already spotless sites for a third or fourth time. From within the ranks of the specialists there were some, like David Whittaker, Robin Richards or Richard Neave and his team of medical artists, who became almost 'regulars' and in whose laboratories we must have become a familiar sight. We owe an enormous debt to them and to all our specialist contributors for their willingness to help with our quests and their patience in explaining their often complex work to a fascinated but far from scientifically educated field archaeologist.

I would like to add my personal thanks to Jane Brayne, our illustrator, whose talents in re-creating the past and skill at interpreting my nightmarish sketches have brought so much life and colour to both the television series and this book. I may have been an archaeologist for nearly thirty years but discovery still fills me with excitement and making *Meet the Ancestors* has at times seemed like a dream come true. I could not have wished for a friendlier production team with whom to share my enthusiasm for the past. I would like to add special thanks to the researchers Tania Lindon, Ben Power and Bucy McDonald.

Finally, I must thank my wife Sue for her patience in coping with the erratic lifestyle that has resulted from our sometimes frantic filming schedules, and apologize to Barnaby for all the times that I have spent either away or hiding on the 'office'. It's playtime now.   *Julian Richards*

PICTURE CREDITS

BBC Worldwide would like to thank the following for providing photographs and for permission to reproduce copyright material. While every effort has been made to trace and acknowledge copyright holders, we would like to apologize if there have been any errors or omissions.

British Museum (photos by Trevor Springett) pp.142, 146, 147; English Life Publications p.195; Luke Finn p.79; Martin Green pp.18–19; Ian Potts pp.2, 54, 55, 62, 63, 94, 107, 122, 125, 159, 166, 167, 169, 194 © BBC; Suffolk County Council pp.132, 134, 138; David Whittaker, Audio-Visual Unit, University of Wales School of Medicine, Cardiff pp.123, 187; Winchester Museum Services p.67 (below).

The computer generated faces on pp. 32, 33, 81, 145, 183, 206 are by Robin Richards. The facial reconstructions are by the following: pp.54, 55, 62, 126 and 127 Richard Neave; p.106 Denise Smith; pp.166 and 167 Caroline Wilkinson. The paintings on pp. 31, 35, 38, 58–9, 82, 150, 151, 190, 191, 202, 207 are by Jane Brayne, © Jane Brayne; the painting on p.103 is by Mark Barden, © Winchester Museum Services; the drawing on p.114 is by Rob Read.

All the other photographs are by Julian Richards, © Julian Richards 1998.